Pioneers of
Human Rights

Profiles · in · History

Cheryl Fisher Phibbs, *Book Editor*

Bruce Glassman, *Vice President*
Bonnie Szumski, *Publisher*
Helen Cothran, *Managing Editor*

GREENHAVEN PRESS
An imprint of Thomson Gale, a part of The Thomson Corporation

THOMSON
™
GALE

Detroit • New York • San Francisco • San Diego • New Haven, Conn.
Waterville, Maine • London • Munich

THOMSON
—————✳—————™
GALE

© 2005 Thomson Gale, a part of The Thomson Corporation.

Thomson and Star Logo are trademarks and Gale and Greenhaven Press are registered trademarks used herein under license.

For more information, contact
Greenhaven Press
27500 Drake Rd.
Farmington Hills, MI 48331-3535
Or you can visit our Internet site at http://www.gale.com

Cover credit: © Jacques M. Chenet/CORBIS. Human rights leader Nelson Mandela holds a
gold key to the city of New York, which was presented to him by Mayor David
Dinkins in 1992.
© Corel Corporation, 81
Jimmy Carter Library, 202
Library of Congress, 46, 106

LIBRARY OF CONGRESS CATALOGING-IN-PUBLICATION DATA

Pioneers of human rights / Cheryl Fisher Phibbs, book editor.
  p. cm. — (Profiles in history)
  Includes bibliographical references and index.
  ISBN 0-7377-2146-4 (lib. : alk. paper)
    1. Human rights workers—Biography. 2. Human rights—History. 3. Human
  rights—History—Sources. I. Phibbs, Cheryl. II. Series.
  JC571.P55 2005
  323'.092'2—dc22   2003068585

Printed in the United States of America

Contents

Foreword   8
Introduction   11

Chapter 1: Mohandas Gandhi: Fighter for Indian Independence

1. Mohandas Gandhi: A Strategy of Nonviolence
by Rebecca Leathem   21
Mohandas Gandhi used nonviolent strategies to work ceaselessly in South Africa and India to improve the rights of Indians.

2. A Sacred Warrior
by Nelson Mandela   31
Gandhi's unique, nonviolent tactics influenced leadership and changed human rights techniques around the world.

3. Gandhi Was Neither Saint nor Politician
by Mohandas Gandhi   38
One political method Gandhi developed was satyagraha. Committed to nonviolence, Gandhi taught satyagraha as the instrument of action, power, and change in India.

4. Gandhi's Message
by Edgar Snow   44
Gandhi shaped the destiny of Indians more than any other leader in the nation's history.

Chapter 2: Nelson Mandela: South African Activist

1. Commitment to Freedom
by C. Stone Brown   53
Nelson Rolihlahla Mandela and others formed a mass movement to challenge the racism of South Africa's apartheid political system.

2. How Prison Influenced Mandela's Commitment to Human Rights
by John Battersby   62
Nelson Mandela discusses his prison experiences and the philosophies that developed there that changed his legacy from a rebel to a hero of the twentieth century.

3. Ending Apartheid
by James Ryan   72
Nelson Mandela's lifelong struggle to overcome apartheid was rewarded with the implementation of a democratic society in South Africa, where he was elected its first president.

4. Human Rights Progress
by Nelson Mandela   79
One of freedom's responsibilities is to ensure the protection of human rights for all peoples, an area that still needs much improvement internationally.

Chapter 3: Freedom Fighters

1. Frederick Douglass: From Slave to Activist
by Richard Conniff   84
Frederick Douglass was one of the foremost leaders against racial injustice.

2. Susan B. Anthony: A Pioneer in Woman's Rights

by Sara Ann McGill 98

Susan B. Anthony fought for woman's rights, including the right to vote, receive equal educational opportunities, and divorce abusive husbands. Her efforts increased support for woman suffrage.

3. Martin Luther King Jr.: Civil Rights Activist

by Russel Moldovan 103

Martin Luther King Jr. led sit-ins and rallies to help break walls of oppression for black citizens around the world before he was martyred for this cause.

4. Iqbal Masih: Martyr for Child Labor

by Timothy Ryan 109

Martyred at the age of twelve for his political activism to end child labor, Iqbal Masih's efforts released thousands of children from bonded labor and changed international business practices.

Chapter 4: Champions for the Oppressed

1. Eleanor Roosevelt: The Human Touch

by Labor Today 116

As the wife of President Franklin D. Roosevelt, Eleanor Roosevelt spent her years in the White House working to better conditions for the poor. Following her husband's death, Roosevelt led the United Nations' first human rights commission.

2. Eva Perón: Out of Poverty and into Activism

by Michael Neill and Laura Sanderson Healy 121

Eva Perón instituted labor laws, minimum wages, and better living conditions for the poor in Argentina.

3. Mary Robinson
by Nance Lucas   127
As head of Ireland and later the UN Commission on Human Rights, Mary Robinson has spent her life championing human rights to government leaders around the world.

Chapter 5: Exposing Human Rights Abuses

1. Tenzin Gyatso: The Dalai Lama of Tibet
by Pico Iyer   141
As Dalai Lama, the spiritual and political leader of Tibet, Tenzin Gyatso speaks out for the liberation of his country from abusive Chinese occupation, which he claims is dismantling Tibet's culture.

2. Harry Wu: Challenging China's Human Rights Record
by Anthony C. LoBaido   153
Harry Wu spent nineteen years in a Chinese labor camp for his outspoken political dissent and now works to document the cruelties and human rights abuses practiced in China's prison system.

3. Wu's Imprisonment Aided His Cause
by Ching-Lee Wu   165
On a third mission into China to document and uncover the abuses of Chinese labor camps, Harry Wu was arrested. It was this arrest that prompted international outcry and protests against the prison system known as the laogai.

4. Natasa Kandic: Fighter Against Human Rights Abuses in Serbia and Kosovo
by Kerry Kennedy Cuomo   169
Natasa Kandic has exposed atrocities committed by Serbian forces during the breakup of Yu-

goslavia. She is a legal pioneer, bringing claims against the abusive governments she exposes.

Chapter 6: Human Rights at Work

1. The UN Commission on Human Rights
by Clark M. Eichelberger   178
The UN Commission on Human Rights works to promote, protect, and strengthen human rights around the world.

2. Amnesty International
by Marie Staunton and Sally Fenn   186
Founded in London in 1961 by a British lawyer named Peter Benenson, Amnesty International began as an organization to rescue political prisoners and other victims of government repression around the world.

3. Jimmy Carter
by Millard Grimes   194
When Jimmy Carter left the U.S. presidency, he set up the Carter Center to focus on humanitarian efforts. He has spent his postpresidential years working to improve human rights conditions around the world.

4. The Carter Center
by Faith McLellan   200
The Carter Center was founded by former U.S. president Jimmy Carter and his wife, Rosalynn, to alleviate human suffering, prevent and resolve conflicts, enhance freedom and democracy for others, and improve global health issues.

Appendix of Documents   206
For Further Research   226
Index   233

Foreword

Historians and other scholars have often argued about which forces are most influential in driving the engines of history. A favorite theory in past ages was that powerful supernatural forces—the gods and/or fate—were deciding factors in earthly events. Modern theories, by contrast, have tended to emphasize more natural and less mysterious factors. In the nineteenth century, for example, the great Scottish historian Thomas Carlyle stated, "No great man lives in vain. The history of the world is but the biography of great men." This was the kernel of what came to be known as the "great man" theory of history, the idea that from time to time an unusually gifted, influential man or woman emerges and pushes the course of civilization in a new direction. According to Carlyle:

> Universal History, the history of what man has accomplished in this world, is at bottom the History of the Great Men who have worked here. They were the leaders of men, these great ones; the modelers . . . of whatsoever the general mass of men contrived to do or to attain; all things that we see standing accomplished in the world are properly the outer material result. . . . The soul of the whole world's history, it may justly be considered, were the history of these [persons].

In this view, individuals such as Moses, Buddha, Augustus, Christ, Constantine, Elizabeth I, Thomas Jefferson, Frederick Douglass, Franklin Roosevelt, and Nelson

Mandela accomplished deeds or promoted ideas that sooner or later reshaped human societies in large portions of the globe.

The great man thesis, which was widely popular in the late 1800s and early 1900s, has since been eclipsed by other theories of history. Some scholars accept the "situational" theory. It holds that human leaders and innovators only react to social situations and movements that develop substantially on their own, through random interactions. In this view, Moses achieved fame less because of his unique personal qualities and more because he wisely dealt with the already existing situation of the Hebrews wandering in the desert in search of a new home.

More widely held, however, is a view that in a sense combines the great man and situational theories. Here, major historical periods and political, social, and cultural movements occur when a group of gifted, influential, and like-minded individuals respond to a situation or need over the course of time. In this scenario, Moses is seen as one of a group of prophets who over the course of centuries established important traditions of monotheism; and over time a handful of ambitious, talented pharaohs led ancient Egypt from its emergence as the world's first nation to its great age of conquest and empire. Likewise, the Greek playwrights Sophocles and Euripides, the Elizabethan playwright Shakespeare, and the American playwright Eugene O'Neill all advanced the art of drama, leading it to its present form.

The books in the Profiles in History series chronicle and examine in detail the leading figures in some of history's most important historical periods and movements. Some, like those covering Egypt's leading pharaohs and the most influential U.S. presidents, deal with national leaders guiding a great people through good times and bad. Other volumes in the series examine the leaders of important, constructive social movements, such as those that sought to abolish slavery in the nineteenth century and fought for human rights in the twentieth century. And some, such as the one on Hitler and his henchmen, profile far less constructive, though no less historically important, groups of leaders.

Each book in the series begins with a detailed essay providing crucial background information on the historical period or movement being covered. The main body of the volume consists of a series of shorter essays, each covering an important individual in that period or movement. Where appropriate, two or more essays are devoted to a particularly influential person. Some of the essays provide biographical information; while others, including primary sources by or about the person, focus in on his or her specific deeds, ideas, speeches, or followers. More primary source documents, providing further detail, appear in an appendix, followed by a chronology of events and a thorough, up-to-date bibliography that guides interested readers to further research. Overall, the volumes of the Profiles in History series offer a balanced view of the march of civilization by demonstrating how certain individuals make history and at the same time are products of the deeds and movements of their predecessors.

Introduction

There are people who stand out in history for their incredible personal sacrifice and tireless efforts to pioneer the cause of human rights. Moved by injustices, these advocates are dedicated to ensuring that fundamental freedoms for every person are promoted and defended. At great personal sacrifice, these pioneers in human rights have made contributions that have shaped the course of history. Their work has changed laws, societies, behavior, and political regimes. Their convictions give hope to others and hold governments accountable to human rights standards as they were internationally defined in 1948.

Who Are the Human Rights Activists?

There is no particular membership, schooling, or initiation ceremony that marks an individual as a human rights defender. The human rights activist is an individual who has made a major commitment to take up the defense and promotion of the human rights of others. He or she is a beacon of hope to the helpless; compelled to pursue freedom for the sake of all citizens.

The term *human rights activist* encompasses a diverse population. Many lawyers are included for taking on the cases of political prisoners or publicly challenging repressive legislation. Samuel Kofi Woods, for example, founded the Catholic Justice and Peace Commission in 1980 to develop ways to meet humanitarian needs during civil war in Liberia. Woods provided legal services to indigents and political prisoners, as well as conducted training on conflict resolution, human rights, and peace building for youth, women, law enforcement, and journalists. Woods's documentation and publication of his government's human rights abuses generated international support for the Liberian people.

Another lawyer, Natasa Kandic, has consistently spoken out against repression, bigotry, and war crimes in war-torn Yugoslavia. She founded the Humanitarian Legal Center to research human rights abuses, and she represents victims before tribunals. She is a bold legal pioneer bringing claims against the Serbian and Montenegran governments, and she provides legal assistance to refugees for citizenship, pension payments, and property ownership rights. Kandic has organized protests, peace campaigns, and produces a weekly column to raise public awareness of human rights issues in a Belgrade newspaper.

Activists also include journalists who use their writing to expose human rights violations. Rana Husseini, a Jordanian journalist, exposed the shame of honor killings. In Jordanian culture, a woman who was raped was considered to have compromised her family's honor. Fathers, brothers, and sons saw it as their duty to avenge the offense, not by pursuing the perpetrators but by murdering the victims: their own daughters, sisters, and mothers. Husseini wrote a series of reports on these killings and launched a campaign to stop them. As a result, she has been threatened and accused of being anti-Islamic, antifamily, and anti-Jordan. The conspiracy of silence regarding this atrocity was broken thanks to this young journalist who risked her life to expose the truth about honor killings.

There are international human rights activist groups such as: Amnesty International, the Citizens Commission on Human Rights, Voice of the Martyrs, Human Rights Watch, and others that operate by organizing individuals around the world. These groups devote significant resources to the promotion and protection of human rights.

By the mid-1970s these groups became a rapidly growing network of highly motivated and increasingly efficient human rights bodies. They recruited and united activists from around the world into powerful citizens' lobbies. Their main purpose is to hold governments to the internationally defined standards of human rights. Those who feel compelled to champion human rights causes are not radical visionaries. They tend to have seen human rights abuses and the results of oppression and desire to answer the cries for help using any tactic that will work.

How They Do It

Getting facts and communicating them to the media, sympathetic governments, or international human rights bodies is usually the activists' first line of defense. Economic, social, cultural, civil, and political rights are a part of their daily work because these areas are so interdependent.

Some activists implement letter-writing campaigns to change laws or initiate public pressure to influence a situation. The World Organization Against Torture boasts over ninety thousand correspondents in the field of human rights ready to intervene on behalf of others. When violating governments have not been sensitive to individual letters or media attention, democratic governments are encouraged to put political or international trade sanctions in place as a means of applying pressure on those countries to implement change. Public demonstrations are another way of exposing human rights issues that need addressing. In June 1989 the

Chinese government ordered the People's Army to turn weapons on students protesting in Tiananmen Square. Although the protest turned into a bloody massacre and drove dissidents into hiding, international outcry put pressure on Chinese trade relations around the world and increased awareness of government oppression in Chinese society.

Public education is a major factor in human rights successes. People must be aware of their rights and conscious of the abuses taking place. For this reason, and to get more visibility and legitimize their work, many activists speak at universities and international meetings.

José Ramos-Horta spent twenty-four years in exile leading an international charge to stop the violence of an Indonesian invasion in East Timor. Ramos-Horta traveled the globe speaking out against these abuses where one-third of the population lost their lives to massacres, starvation, epidemics, and terror.

> I thought of the spirits of those in East Timor, telling me to fight on. I worked on the cause of East Timor as a full-time job, twenty-four hours a day almost. I had no money, but I would get in the bus and go anywhere in the U.S. to talk. I got an invitation to go to Milwaukee—I went and spoke there. One day I went all the way to Chicago because a very kind activist managed to get my name included in a big conference in a fancy hotel.[1]

Ramos-Horta says winning the Nobel Peace Prize in 1996 gave him access to the international governments and the media. "I tell you, I was so sad, so alone. I went to Washington and met with Senators Patrick Leahy, and Tom Harkin, and people in the State Department like Thomas Pickering. I spoke at the National Press Club, and appeared on program after program for NBC, ABC, Night Line, and CNN."[2] Ramos-Horta said hundreds of thousands of people made phone calls and sent Internet messages that helped to change the tide. Because of his appeals the United Nations sent in troops to stop the violence, and in 1999, after twenty-four years of working in exile, he returned home to a free and independent East Timor.

In the United States many universities have implemented college programs on human rights to increase awareness and raise up defenders of this cause. Juan Méndez runs the human rights program at the University of Notre Dame. Méndez claims, "Without academic organizations that can train and professionalize activists in different parts of the world, the human rights movement cannot continue to grow and improve. We must bring in new generations of people. Knowledge has to be transmitted."[3]

Overcoming Government Obstacles

Many times, the crimes questioned by human rights activists are a direct result of governmental abuses. One anonymous activist in Sudan says,

> It is certainly to the government's benefit that people don't know much about the laws, because then people will not demand any rights. This is one reason why it would be difficult for me to reveal my name. Those whom the government suspects of working on human rights are arrested, often tortured in ghost houses (which are unknown detention centers) or, if one is lucky, put in prison for an undetermined period of time. Just recently we had a journalist arrested who was kept in jail for a short while, comparatively—only two months. But he was tortured: both knees broken and his feet burned. The police didn't want to release him because they were afraid that his family would object. They kept him until his feet healed. There are so many incidents of this sort, as well as disappearances. The best way to stop these abuses is for people to be aware of their rights.[4]

Human rights defenders seem to be among a small

minority willing to stand up to these oppressive political systems, measuring their effectiveness when international covenants, laws, and conditions are established to better human rights.

At What Cost?

One attribute all human rights activists seem to share is that they believe so deeply in freedom, they are prepared to risk everything, including their lives, in its defense. Threat of arrest, torture, and even death does not silence them. To advance the cause of human rights, these advocates wrestle with political authorities and powerful institutions. They have become the victims of violence at the hands of governments, security forces, international drug gangs, and armed dissidents.

Victimizers use a wide range of strategies in their efforts to suppress human rights activists. Deterrents have included detention without trial in prisons and psychiatric institutions. Activists have been harassed, searched without warrant, physically and mentally tortured, and have mysteriously disappeared. Many have been executed by death squads and vigilante groups. They live under surveillance, and have been denied passports and visas. The list of harassment is limited only by the imagination of the oppressors.

Samuel Kofi Woods says that since 1980 he has slept in a different place every night for security reasons, often sleeping only two hours at a time. "It doesn't feel good because it doesn't make you a normal person. But you are propelled because you are doing a good deed. You are trying to sacrifice so that other people can survive, so they see hope and meaning in living."[5]

Individuals who expose human rights abuses are not offered witness protection. They are always at risk because challenging those who wield power is always dangerous. As they work in the face of danger, personal risk becomes a lifestyle—yet they pursue their causes with incredible conviction.

An individual moved by injustice is the greatest driving force for the cause of human rights. Human rights pioneers share a general conviction to give others hope and meaning for their lives.

One anonymous activist describes why he works for human rights in the face of great personal danger. He saw every kind of abuse, from harassment to false imprisonment, to beatings, to rape, to politically motivated murder by authorities and others, yet he continued to work for human rights in the face of great personal danger. As these atrocities became part of his personal experience, he learned never to take his own freedom for granted.

Most pioneers in human rights are motivated because they have either been a victim of human rights abuses or touched by the plight of those victimized by abuse.

Dianna Ortizan, an Ursuline nun from New Mexico, tells that crimes against her motivated her to fight the U.S. government. As a missionary in Guatemala in the early 1980s, Ortizan was abducted, tortured, and gang-raped by agents of the Guatemalan government. When Ortizan tried to get the U.S. government's help in identifying her torturers, she felt brutalized again.

Ortizan says,

> I cannot forget those who suffered with me and died in that clandestine prison. I stand with the Guatemalan people. I demand the right to a future built on truth and justice. I know what few U.S. citizens know: what it is to be an innocent civilian, and to be accused, interrogated, and tortured, to have my own government eschew my claims for justice and actively destroy my character because my case causes political problems for them. I know what it means to wait in the dark for torture, and what it is to wait in the dark for truth.[6]

Ortizan's work for human rights supports her belief

that behind every victim, there is an individual, a family, a community, and a world that is also deeply affected.

Bobby Mueller, an advocate of veterans and victims of war and a Nobel Peace Prize winner for his campaign to ban land mines said,

> Courage for me means swimming against the tide. To go on in the face of adversity. To be willing to expose yourself to failure and ridicule. You have to be conscious of the fact that you're at risk and aware of what you can lose—to then go forward is a courageous act. You can lose reputation and money, its security and possibly your life. You're doing it not because you're gonna get applauded at some point down the road, or rewarded, but because it's right.[7]

Their Contributions

Pioneers in human rights have made contributions that have shaped the course of history. Andrey Sakharov, a Russian physicist, became a public witness for human rights and is attributed with crippling communism in the Soviet Union. Mohandas Gandhi's efforts to rally a nation in unified protest unsettled the English rule of India and made human rights a global issue. Nelson Mandela dedicated his life to abolishing the unjust political system of apartheid in South Africa, a nation which now celebrates democracy because of his efforts; and a twelve-year-old boy sold into bonded slavery when he was only four years old, Iqbal Masih, was martyred after calling attention to child slave labor in the Pakistani carpet industry. Masih's death improved labor laws and international business practices that crossed global industry boundaries. These are just a few of the pioneers who have created human rights as an ideological force to be reckoned with. They have been prophets in a dangerous wilderness creating tactics and courageously forging a path for others to follow more clearly.

A U.S. State Department bulletin issued in February

1986 addressing human rights states, "We have learned from history that the cause of peace and human freedom is indivisible. Respect for human rights is essential to true peace on earth."[8] The human rights pioneers who adopt and pursue this challenge are, at great personal risk, making a positive difference for others that will continue to change history.

Notes

1. Quoted in Kerry Kennedy Cuomo, *Speak Truth to Power.* New York: Crown, 2000, p. 165.
2. Quoted in Cuomo, *Speak Truth to Power*, p. 79.
3. Quoted in Cuomo, *Speak Truth to Power*, p. 182.
4. Quoted in Cuomo, *Speak Truth to Power*, p. 182.
5. Quoted in George M. Anderson, "Liberia and Human Rights," *America*, May 14, 2001, p. 7.
6. Quoted in Cuomo, *Speak Truth to Power*, p. 51.
7. Quoted in Cuomo, *Speak Truth to Power* p. 91.
8. U.S. Department of State, *Safeguarding Human Rights*, Washington, DC: U.S. Government Printing Office, February 1986, p. 87.

CHAPTER

1

Profiles · in · History

Mohandas Gandhi: Fighter for Indian Independence

Mohandas Gandhi: A Strategy of Nonviolence

Rebecca Leathem

Mohandas Gandhi transformed human rights in India through his revolutionary leadership style and commitment to nonviolence. In this viewpoint Rebecca Leathem presents some of the peaceful methods Gandhi used to attack the unjust caste system while India was under British rule in the early 1900s.

Gandhi's strategies of nonviolence were derived from his quest for spirituality. It was Gandhi's opinion that if he could persuade his followers to strive for peace and harmony, and to accept brutality from British soldiers and police without retaliation, their revolt would be successful. Gandhi used fasts, petitions, demonstrations, strikes, and prayer as weapons against the rule of the British government. He promoted the use of homespun cloth to oppose textile imports from Britain and swapped his English suit for the traditional Indian loincloth as a way to show support for Indian culture. He urged Indians to make themselves worthy of equality by becoming educated.

Leathem is an editorial co-coordinator for *Business Class*, a magazine for business and professional women.

Rebecca Leathem, "Mahatma Gandhi," *Business Asia*, February 15, 1999. Copyright © 1999 by First Charlton Communications, Ltd. Reproduced by permission.

❦ ❦ ❦

On January 30, 1948, a few months after the independence of India in which he had played the chief role, Mohandas Gandhi walked to his evening prayers in Delhi. A young man named Nathuram Godse pushed his way through the crowd around Gandhi and crouched to kiss his feet. As Godse was pulled away by guards, he drew a gun and shot Gandhi three times. Gandhi fell dying, his final words, "Hai Rama!"—"O God!"

So died a great Asian, also known in India and around the world by the title "Mahatma", a Hindi word meaning "of great soul" or "revered one".

Lord Mountbatten, the last British Viceroy of India, said Gandhi would go down in history as "on par with Buddha and Jesus Christ", and Albert Einstein, philosopher and Nobel Prize science winner, said "Generations to come will scarcely believe that such a one as this ever in flesh and blood walked upon this earth." Fifty years after Gandhi's death the nation he created is the world's largest democracy, with the secret ballot, a free press and an independent judiciary.

Karamchand Mohandas Gandhi was born on October 2, 1869, the third son and the last of four children of well-to-do Hindu parents, at Porbandor on the north-west coast of India. His family was of the Bania sub-caste, traditionally working merchants and traders. When Gandhi was born, India was the "jewel in the crown" of the British Empire. . . .

Gandhi grew up in a traditional Hindu family. His mother Putili Ba strongly influenced his moral, social and religious beliefs.

Gandhi's father was Dewan (chief minister) to the princely ruler of Porbandor. This was a traditional post for the Gandhi family, which had high expectations that the young Mohandas would eventually take the role.

When the family moved to Rajkot, where Gandhi's father became assessor in a court which settled local disputes, Gandhi had his first experience of colonial power as Rajkot was a local centre of British rule.

At the age of 13 Gandhi was married to Kasturbi, also 13 years old and the daughter of a merchant. Kasturbi was illiterate but hardworking and level headed. Relations between her and Gandhi were strained at times, but they had four sons in 12 years. Later Gandhi took a vow of sexual abstinence. One reason was a quest for spiritual purity, another was that news of his father's death arrived when he was in bed with his wife and he believed penance was needed.

At the age of 19 his family sent him to London to study law, hoping this would prepare him to later take his father's government position.

In London, Gandhi changed his tropical cottons for a dark suit and bowler hat and studied hard for five years. He read widely outside his law books, including works by the Russian novelist Leo Tolstoy and English moralist John Ruskin. He also attended meetings of the Theosophical Society which discussed religions and philosophies. Gandhi began to develop his own philosophy of Ahimsa and Satya (Non-violence and Truth).

South Africa

After graduation in 1893, Gandhi went to South Africa to escape the demands of his family. There he became legal adviser to a group of Indian merchants and stayed for 21 years. South Africa then comprised states under British (Natal and the Cape Colony) and Dutch (Transvaal and the Orange Free State) rule. The colonial policies of racial discrimination led Gandhi to his first acts of satyagraha, or passive resistance, against laws restricting the lives and rights of nonwhites. Most Indians in South Africa were indentured immigrant labourers. They were tied to a single employer until their contracts expired. Then they were able to buy freedom, but only in the British areas did they have the right to vote.

Gandhi was particularly angered by the restrictions on the Transvaal Indian community of 12,000. They were limited in land ownership, could not go out after 9 P.M., could not vote and had to pay special taxes. Gandhi set about reforms, but not by confrontation. Instead, he declared Indians must make themselves worthy of equality.

The Boers, the majority community of Dutch descent, claimed Indians were dirty, dishonest and ignorant. Gandhi's advice to his fellow Indians was that they should respond with fastidious hygiene, education and be scrupulous in business. The Boers said Indians were unworthy of voting rights, the excuse being divisions within the community, especially Hindu-Muslim differences. Gandhi advised Indians to unite, regardless of religion.

In 1894, Gandhi opposed legislation in British-ruled Natal which was intended to deprive Indians there of the right to vote for the National Assembly. He formed a committee, wrote to newspapers and petitioned officials. Gandhi collected 10,000 signatures against the legislation but had only a moral victory. The Assembly passed a law without mentioning Indians directly, but achieving the same discrimination.

The treatment of indentured Indian labourers was another Gandhi target. He petitioned government and wrote newspaper articles about their plight. When they had finished work contracts the labourers had to choose between returning to India, beginning a new indentured contract, or buying freedom at a cost equivalent to a year's pay. After many Gandhi petitions and articles, the British Viceroy of India complained to London about the treatment of his Indian subjects in South Africa. As a result the annual "tax" was reduced to about one month's pay, an improvement which proved Gandhi's actions and arguments had some effect in London, as well as in South Africa and India.

Although the Indian civil rights struggle progressed, the white community's racist treatment of Indians did not change.

Gandhi's next political target was a Transvaal law compelling Indians to register and be fingerprinted. About 3,000 Indians held a protest meeting at which a Muslim merchant vowed to defy the law. Gandhi warned that this would risk jail and fines, but the entire audience vowed to resist. As a result only a few hundred of the 13,000 Indian community registered. Gandhi and his supporters were sentenced to two months in prison.

As the cells filled with resisters, the government retreated, saying they would be released if they agreed to register voluntarily. Gandhi agreed to this compromise and many Indians followed his example. However, when the government broke its promise Gandhi began another satyagraha and thousands burned their registration cards outside a mosque in Johannesburg.

When Gandhi left South Africa in 1914, General Jan Smuts, later Prime Minister of South Africa, said "The saint has left our shores. I hope forever."

Spinning Wheel

Gandhi returned to India from his long political apprenticeship with social and economic views which seemed radical there. However, the Raj was beginning to reform.

For Gandhi, the political struggle in India was closely connected with economic, social and communal problems. He promoted the use of home-spun cloth in opposition to textiles imported from Britain. He also attacked the concept of untouchability and declared that Untouchables, the lowest caste, be called Harijans, "the children of God".

"Swaraj", self-rule, was his ultimate aim but the omens in the 1920s were not good. Commodity prices and taxes soared and strikes, epidemics and terrorist attacks were common. In response, the British declared political crimes could be tried in secret and without a jury.

Gandhi's reaction was to call for a general strike and days of prayer. Muslims and Hindus marched together, waving banners and chanting. In the northern city of Amritsar, capital of the Sikhs, an English schoolteacher was assaulted. The British Commander, General Dyer, banned public meetings. Not knowing of this order, about 5,000 Indians gathered in a square and on Dyer's orders troops fired on the crowd. The death toll was 379, with 1,137 wounded.

Gandhi blamed the violence on himself and fasted for three days, the first of his many political fasts. He decided that his non-violent strategies were unworkable until all Indians understood them. He set about teaching, with the Indian National Congress as his platform.

Most Congress members were well-to-do English speakers who wore European clothes and had been educated overseas. Their endless talk seemed to lead to little action, so Gandhi began changing Congress style and members. He symbolically rejected British rule by swapping his English suits for the dhoti, the traditional loincloth of the Indian labourer, and reverting to his native language, Gujarati. To spread his strategy of non-cooperation with British rule, Gandhi founded the National Volunteer Corps. Among those who joined was Jawaharlal Nehru, son of the president of the Congress and later the first Prime Minister of India. Nehru followed Gandhi's pilgrimage across India as he took his ideas to the millions. Everywhere they went volunteers taught villagers how to spin and weave their raw cotton into cloth. This symbolic action became a vivid image of indian nationalism and the Gandhian politics of non-violence. The spinning wheel is the central symbol of the national flag of modern India.

As the independence movement gathered pace and passion, and began to disrupt British control, the government arrested volunteers and congress members. By March 1920, some 30,000 were in prison and Gandhi was charged with sedition. At his trial he stated, "I submit to the highest penalty that can be inflicted on me for what in law is a deliberate crime, but what appears to me to be the highest duty of a citizen." He was sentenced to six years, but was released after three years following surgery for appendicitis.

While Gandhi was in prison the independence movement split along Hindu-Muslim lines. The Muslim League, headed by Mohammed Ali Jinnah, left the Indian National Congress. The tensions between the two religious groups led to riots. Gandhi vowed to fast until relations between the two groups improved. Hindu and Muslim leaders came to his bedside to pledge harmony. Gandhi's fast lasted three weeks. The unity lasted only a few years.

In 1927, Congress declared itself ready to rule India, although Britain decided not to consider independence until 1929. Within the Congress there was great debate on what form independence should take. Gandhi declared he would continue national non-cooperation campaigns unless India was given self-governing Dominion status.

In 1930, Jawaharlal Nehru became, at the age of 41, president of Congress. He read a Declaration of Independence and raised an Indian flag. But India remained under British rule as it had been for a century.

A Symbolic Victory

Gandhi's next tactic was to defy the tax on salt, an essential commodity which was a government monopoly. He led a 322-km protest march—a skinny, brown, half naked 60-year-old man with a bamboo stave and a few followers, including Nehru, walking 20 kilometres a day. To the crowds along the way he declared, "Either I shall return with what I want, or else my dead body will float in the ocean."

On April 6, 1930, the marchers reached the Arabian Sea, performed a purification ritual, gathered some salt and thereby broke the law. Thousands of Indians soon followed his lead and gathered sea salt. They also boycotted shops stocking British goods.

The colonial Government waited for the political heat and dust to recede but it persisted. Gandhi and Nehru were imprisoned. Some 2,500 Gandhi volunteers gathered to raid a saltworks. Hundreds of Indian police, under British officers, clubbed them as they advanced but none resisted. The news of violence met by non-violence spread around the world. Gandhi began to be a global name.

A few months later the British offered to talk with Gandhi about constitutional reform. He first insisted on repeal of the salt laws. Gandhi called off the campaign of civil disobedience and went to London to listen to the British. It was another symbolic victory—the humble law student returned as a national leader and international figure. The talks led to nothing acceptable to Gandhi. He wrote to the Viceroy: "On bended knee I asked for bread, and you gave me stone instead."

Gandhi resumed his campaigns, was sent back to jail and Congress was outlawed. However, real reforms did finally begin four years later. Britain passed the historic Government of India Act, which allowed large areas to govern themselves with a degree of local independence.

Real power still remained under British control in Delhi, but Congress took the limited opportunity and won seats in the self-governing provinces. Ominously, the Muslim League won only five per cent of the Muslim vote and its leader, Mohammed Ali Jinnah, predicted a "Hindu" dictatorship over Muslims.

When World War II began in 1939, war of another sort began in India. To tighten wartime control in India the British again restricted Indian freedoms. Another satyagraha movement began and Gandhi, Nehru and 20,000 followers were jailed. In 1941, the campaign died away and Gandhi was released.

When war came to Asia, with Japan's Pacific invasions in 1942, Gandhi and Nehru offered Indian help to the British war effort but only as a free country. The British had little choice and so offered Dominion status after the war. However, since the proposal would have also allowed any religious group, province or princely state to secede (and maybe stay under British rule) Gandhi refused the offer. He began his "quit India" campaign and was jailed again. To be with her husband in jail, Kasturbi made an anti-British speech and was also arrested.

The popular response to the jailing of the apostle of non-violence was violent. Post offices, railway stations and banks were burned. About 600 people were killed and 36,000 imprisoned. Gandhi began another protest fast. Terrified that Gandhi would die, the Viceroy, Field Marshall Wavell, sent doctors to watch over him. Gandhi survived but his wife died in February 1944. In May, on the eve of the Allied invasion of German-occupied Europe, Gandhi was released from jail for the last time.

Last Days

In February 1947 Admiral Lord Louis Mountbatten, a relative of the British royal family, was appointed the last

Viceroy of India. He was glamourous but incompetent. The timing of many of his actions remains controversial. In essence, his critics say he moved too fast for safety.

Muslim leaders insisted that an independent Muslim state be created. The Congress Party conceded the territories Muslims wanted—north-west and north-east India became Pakistan, a nation physically divided by 1,500 kilometres of India. Independence for both nations came at midnight on August 14, 1947.

The achievement of independence created far more violence than the struggle for it. In the partition, Hindus fled Pakistan and Muslims fled India. About one million people died in the greatest mass movement in modern history as seven million people left their old homes for new nations. Gandhi saw his life of non-violence culminating in mass violence. He could only react with fasting. In his last days, despair often exceeded elation.

India was independent but endangered. Between fasts, and between Hindu-Muslim truces, Gandhi visited the scenes of riot destruction, met refugees, talked with Nehru, now Prime Minister, and grew weaker and sadder. He was 78. An extremist Hindu conspiracy to kill him was discovered and Gandhi declared, "If I die by the bullet of a mad man I must do so smiling. Should such a thing happen to me, you are not to shed one tear." Ten days later he was assassinated by a Hindu fanatic opposed to partition and millions wept.

Half a century on, India's independence and democracy are Gandhi's monuments. Although modern India—where the computer is almost as common as the spinning wheel—is not in his home-spun image, it is the world's largest democracy—an achievement for which his lifelong sacrifice for freedom laid the foundations.

A Sacred Warrior

Nelson Mandela

According to Nelson Mandela, leader of the African National Congress, Gandhi developed a blueprint for a new social order in the area of human rights that paved the way for international liberation. In the following article Mandela describes Gandhi as a revolutionary who mobilized people against the governments that violated their human rights. Mandela discusses Gandhi's extraordinary leadership style, saying Gandhi inspired group interest, justice, morality, and nonviolence during a time when these practices were unpopular.

Mandela served as South Africa's first democratically elected president from 1994 until 1999 and has authored several books.

🐾 🐾 🐾

India is Gandhi's country of birth; South Africa his country of adoption. He was both an Indian and a South African citizen. Both countries contributed to his intellectual and moral genius, and he shaped the liberatory movements in both colonial theaters.

He is the archetypal anticolonial revolutionary. His strategy of noncooperation, his assertion that we can be dominated only if we cooperate with our dominators, and his nonviolent resistance inspired anticolonial and antiracist movements internationally in our century.

Both Gandhi and I suffered colonial oppression, and both of us mobilized our respective peoples against governments that violated our freedoms.

The Gandhian influence dominated freedom struggles on the African continent right up to the 1960s because of the power it generated and the unity it forged among the apparently powerless. Nonviolence was the official stance of all major African coalitions, and the South African A.N.C. [African National Congress] remained implacably opposed to violence for most of its existence.

Gandhi remained committed to nonviolence, . . . [but] never ruled out violence absolutely and unreservedly. He conceded the necessity of arms in certain situations. He said, "Where choice is set between cowardice and violence, I would advise violence. . . . I prefer to use arms in defense of honor rather than remain the vile witness of dishonor. . . ."

Violence and nonviolence are not mutually exclusive; it is the predominance of the one or the other that labels a struggle.

Gandhi arrived in South Africa in 1893 at the age of 23. Within a week he collided head on with racism. His immediate response was to flee the country that so degraded people of color, but then his inner resilience overpowered him with a sense of mission, and he stayed to redeem the dignity of the racially exploited, to pave the way for the liberation of the colonized the world over and to develop a blueprint for a new social order.

He left 21 years later, a near maha atma (great soul). There is no doubt in my mind that by the time he was violently removed from our world, he had transited into that state.

No Ordinary Leader

He was no ordinary leader. There are those who believe he was divinely inspired, and it is difficult not to believe with them. He dared to exhort nonviolence in a time when the violence of Hiroshima and Nagasaki[1] had exploded on us; he exhorted morality when science, technology and the capitalist order had made it redundant; he replaced self-interest with group interest without minimizing the importance of self. In fact, the interdependence of the social and the personal is at the heart of his philosophy. He seeks the simultaneous and interactive development of the moral person and the moral society.

His philosophy of Satyagraha is both a personal and a social struggle to realize the Truth, which he identifies as God, the Absolute Morality. He seeks this Truth, not in isolation, self-centeredly, but with the people. He said, "I want to find God, and because I want to find God, I have to find God along with other people. I don't believe I can find God alone, if I did, I would be running to the Himalayas to find God in some cave there. But since I believe that nobody can find God alone, I have to work with people. I have to take them with me. Alone I can't come to Him.". . .

Awakening

His awakening came on the hilly terrain of the so-called Bambata Rebellion, where as a passionate British patriot, he led his Indian stretcher-bearer corps to serve the Empire, but British brutality against the Zulus roused his soul against violence as nothing had done before. He determined, on that battlefield, to wrest himself of all material attachments and devote himself completely and totally to eliminating violence and serv-

1. cities in Japan targeted by atomic bombs on August 6, 1945, which helped to end World War II but left massive biological and natural destruction as a consequence

ing humanity. The sight of wounded and whipped Zulus, mercilessly abandoned by their British persecutors, so appalled him that he turned full circle from his admiration for all things British to celebrating the indigenous and ethnic. He resuscitated the culture of the colonized and the fullness of Indian resistance against the British; he revived Indian handicrafts and made these into an economic weapon against the colonizer in his call for swadeshi—the use of one's own and the boycott of the oppressor's products, which deprive the people of their skills and their capital.

A great measure of world poverty today and African poverty in particular is due to the continuing dependence on foreign markets for manufactured goods, which undermines domestic production and dams up domestic skills, apart from piling up unmanageable foreign debts. Gandhi's insistence on self-sufficiency is a basic economic principle that, if followed today, could contribute significantly to alleviating Third World poverty and stimulating development.

Gandhi predated Frantz Fanon and the black-consciousness movements in South Africa and the U.S. by more than a half-century and inspired the resurgence of the indigenous intellect, spirit and industry.

Gandhi rejects the Adam Smith notion of human nature as motivated by self-interest and brute needs and returns us to our spiritual dimension with its impulses for nonviolence, justice and equality.

He exposes the fallacy of the claim that everyone can be rich and successful provided they work hard. He points to the millions who work themselves to the bone and still remain hungry. He preaches the gospel of leveling down, of emulating the kisan (peasant), not the zamindar (landlord), for "all can be kisans, but only a few zamindars."

He stepped down from his comfortable life to join

The Magnitude of Gandhi

In The Life and Death of Mahatma Gandhi, *Robert Payne reveals Gandhi's mission in life and how the extent of his greatness surpasses history.*

Gandhi showed that non-violent resistance was at least as powerful as guns; and he opened the way for more enduring conquests. Through him men have learned that no government, even the most tyrannical, is immune from non-violent resistance in the hands of determined and fearless men. No power on earth can resist the aroused consciences of men once they are disciplined and prepared to die for their beliefs. Gandhi was prepared to die: this was his most powerful weapon. . . .

A few months before his death he watched India being torn apart into two bleeding fragments, and he may have known that his fight for Hindu-Muslim unity was doomed to failure. The agony of his last days was terrible to watch: to the very end he struggled against the partition of his country. Yet he had set the wheel in motion, and his triumphs were at least as memorable as his failures. He brought freedom and independence to India and he changed men's minds.

Most of the men who have profoundly affected history have possessed one-track minds: they have one aim, and spend their energies in obtaining it. Gandhi's aims were various. His private aim was to see God face to face. . . . His public aim was to topple the British Raj [rule] and to bring about the freedom and independence of India, and at the same time he wanted to bring about a transformation of Indian society to make her more worthy of her freedom.

Robert Payne, *The Life and Death of Mahatma Gandhi.* New York: E.P. Dutton, 1969, pp. 14–15.

the masses on their level to seek equality with them. "I can't hope to bring about economic equality. . . . I have to reduce myself to the level of the poorest of the poor."

From his understanding of wealth and poverty came his understanding of labor and capital, which led him to the solution of trusteeship based on the belief that there is no private ownership of capital; it is given in trust for redistribution and equalization. Similarly, while recognizing differential aptitudes and talents, he holds that these are gifts from God to be used for the collective good.

He seeks an economic order, alternative to the capitalist and communist, and finds this in sarvodaya [a movement for spiritual self development which promotes peace and community].

He rejects [naturalist Charles] Darwin's survival of the fittest, Adam Smith's laissez-faire and Karl Marx's thesis of a natural antagonism between capital and labor, and focuses on the interdependence between the two.

He believes in the human capacity to change and wages Satyagraha against the oppressor, not to destroy him but to transform him, that he cease his oppression and join the oppressed in the pursuit of Truth. . . .

Gandhi remains today the only complete critique of advanced industrial society. Others have criticized its totalitarianism but not its productive apparatus. He is not against science and technology, but he places priority on the right to work and opposes mechanization to the extent that it usurps this right. Large-scale machinery, he holds, concentrates wealth in the hands of one man who tyrannizes the rest. He favors the small machine; he seeks to keep the individual in control of his tools, to maintain an interdependent love relation between the two, as a cricketer with his bat or Krishna with his flute. Above all, he seeks to liberate the individual from his alienation to the machine and restore morality to the productive process.

As we find ourselves in jobless economies, societies in which small minorities consume while the masses starve, we find ourselves forced to rethink the rationale of our current globalization and to ponder the Gandhian alternative.

At a time when [psychoanalyst Sigmund] Freud was liberating sex, Gandhi was reining it in; when Marx was pitting worker against capitalist, Gandhi was reconciling them; when the dominant European thought had dropped God and soul out of the social reckoning, he was centralizing society in God and soul; at a time when the colonized had ceased to think and control, he dared to think and control; and when the ideologies of the colonized had virtually disappeared, he revived them and empowered them with a potency that liberated and redeemed.

Gandhi Was Neither Saint nor Politician

Mohandas Gandhi

In a rebuttal to an article criticizing him for mixing politics and religion, Mohandas Gandhi, in the following excerpt, paints a detailed self-portrait that highlights his personal philosophies. Although Gandhi claims not to be a politician, he says he wrestles with politics because it cannot be avoided. He comments that he allies himself with the weaker party and teaches direct, harmless action to make the Indian people feel capable of defying the physical oppressiveness of the British government.

🌺 🌺 🌺

A kind friend has sent me the following cutting from the April [1920 issue] of the *East and West:*

> Mr Gandhi has the reputation of a saint but it seems that the politician in him often dominates his decisions. He has been making great use of *hartals* [general shutdowns] and there can be no gainsaying that under his direction *hartal* is becoming a powerful po-

M.K. Gandhi, *Non-Violent Resistance*. New York: Schocken Books, 1951.

litical weapon for uniting the educated and the un-educated on a single question of the day. The *hartal* is not without its disadvantages. It is teaching direct action, and direct action however potent does not work for unity. Is Mr Gandhi quite sure that he is serving the highest behests of *ahimsa* [a Buddhist and Hindu doctrine claiming the sacredness of all living creatures; it urges nonviolence] harmlessness? His proposal to commemorate the shooting at Jalianwala Bagh [a large public space enclosed on three sides by buildings with only one exit became a mass graveyard when a British Military Commander closed the exit and ordered soldiers to fire machine guns into a pro-testing crowd to terrorize them into submission; thousands were slaughtered] is not likely to promote concord. It is a tragic incident into which our Gov-ernment was betrayed, but is the memory of its bit-terness worth retaining? Can we not commemorate the event by raising a temple of peace, to help the widows and orphans, to bless the souls of those who died without knowing why? The world is full of pol-iticians and petti-foggers who, in the name of patrio-tism, poison the inner sweetness of man and, as a re-sult, we have wars and feuds and such shameless slaughter as turned Jalianwala Bagh into a shambles. Shall we not now try for a larger symbiosis such as Buddha and Christ preached, and bring the world to breathe and prosper together? Mr Gandhi seemed destined to be the apostle of such a movement, but circumstances are forcing him to seek the way of rais-ing resistances and group unities. He may yet take up the larger mission of uniting the world.

I have given the whole of the quotation. As a rule I do not notice criticism of me or my methods except when thereby I acknowledge a mistake or enforce still further the principles criticized. I have a double reason for noticing the extract. For, not only do I hope further to elucidate the principles I hold dear, but I want to show my regard for the author of the criticism whom I know and whom I have admired for many years for the

singular beauty of his character. The critic regrets to
see in me a politician whereas he expected me to be a
saint. Now I think that the word *saint* should be ruled
out of present life. It is too sacred a word to be lightly
applied to anybody, much less to one like myself who
claims only to be a humble searcher after truth, knows
his limitations, makes mistakes, never hesitates to admit
them when he makes them, and frankly confesses that
he, like a scientist, is making experiments about some
'of the eternal verities' of life, but cannot even claim to
be a scientist because he can show no tangible proof of
scientific accuracy in his methods or such tangible results of his experiments as modern science demands.
But though by disclaiming sainthood I disappoint the
critic's expectations, I would have him to give up his regrets by answering him that the politician in me has
never dominated a single decision of mine, and if I
seem to take part in politics, it is only because politics
encircle us today like the coil of a snake from which one
cannot get out, no matter how much one tries. I wish
therefore to wrestle with the snake, as I have been doing with more or less success consciously since 1894,
unconsciously, as I have now discovered, ever since
reaching years of discretion. Quite selfishly, as I wish to
live in peace in the midst of a bellowing storm howling
round me, I have been experimenting with myself and
my friends by introducing religion into politics. Let me
explain what I mean by religion. It is not the Hindu religion, which I certainly prize above all other religions,
but the religion which transcends Hinduism, which
changes one's very nature, which binds one indissolubly
to the truth within and which ever purifies. It is the
permanent element in human nature which counts no
cost too great in order to find full expression and which
leaves the soul utterly restless until it has found itself,
known its Maker and appreciated the true correspon-

dence between the Maker and itself.

It was in that religious spirit that I came upon *hartal*. I wanted to show that it is not a knowledge of letters that would give India consciousness of herself, or that would bind the educated together. The *hartal* illuminated the whole of India as if by magic on the 6th of April, 1919. And had it not been for the interruption of the 10th of April, brought about by Satan whispering fear into the ears of a Government conscious of its own wrong and inciting to anger a people that were prepared for it by utter distrust of the Government, India would have risen to an unimaginable height. The *hartal* had not only been taken up by the great masses of people in a truly religious spirit but it was intended to be a prelude to a series of direct actions.

An Ally of the Weak

But my critic deplores direct action. For, he says, "it does not work for unity." I join issue with him. Never has anything been done on this earth without direct action. I rejected the word *passive resistance* because of its insufficiency and its being interpreted as a weapon of the weak. It was direct action in South Africa which told and told so effectively that it converted General [Jan] Smuts to sanity. He was in 1906 the most relentless opponent of Indian aspirations. In 1914, he took pride in doing tardy justice by removing from the Statute Book of the Union a disgraceful measure which, in 1909 he had told Lord Morley, would be never removed, for he then said South Africa would never tolerate repeal of a measure which was twice passed by the Transvaal Legislature. But what is more, direct action sustained for eight years left behind it not only no bitterness but the very Indians who put up such a stubborn fight against General Smuts ranged themselves round his banner in 1915 and fought under him in East Africa. It was direct action in Cham-

paran which removed an agelong grievance. A meek submission when one is chafing under a disability or a grievance which one would gladly see removed, not only does
not make for unity, but makes the weak party acid, angry
and prepares him for an opportunity to explode. By ally-
ing myself with the weak party, by teaching him direct,
firm, but harmless action, I make him feel strong and capable of defying the physical might. He feels braced for
the struggle, regains confidence in himself and knowing
that the remedy lies with himself, ceases to harbour the
spirit of revenge and learns to be satisfied with a redress
of the wrong he is seeking to remedy.

It is working along the same line that I have ventured
to suggest a memorial about Jalianwala Bagh. The
writer in *East and West* has ascribed to me a proposal
which has never once crossed my mind. He thinks that
I want "to commemorate the shooting at Jalianwala
Bagh". Nothing can be further from my thought than to
perpetuate the memory of a black deed. I dare say that
before we have come to our own we shall have a repeti-
tion of the tragedy and I will prepare the nation for it by
treasuring the memory of the innocent dead. The widows and the orphans have been and are being helped,
but we cannot "bless the souls of those who died without knowing why," if we will not acquire the ground
which has been hallowed by innocent blood and there
erect a suitable memorial for them. It is not to serve, if
I can help it, as a reminder of a foul deed, but it shall
serve as an encouragement to the nation that it is better
to die helpless and unarmed and as victims rather than
as tyrants. I would have the future generations remember that we who witnessed the innocent dying did not
ungratefully refuse to cherish their memory.

What was the larger 'symbiosis' that Buddha and
Christ preached? Buddha fearlessly carried the war into
the enemy's camp and brought down on its knees an

arrogant priesthood. Christ drove out the money-changers from the temple of Jerusalem and drew down curses from Heaven upon the hypocrites and the pharisees. Both were for intensely direct action. But even as Buddha and Christ chastized they showed unmistakable gentleness and love behind every act of theirs. They would not raise a finger against their enemies, but would gladly surrender themselves rather than the truth for which they lived. Buddha would have died resisting the priesthood, if the majesty of his love had not proved to be equal to the task of bending the priesthood. Christ died on the cross with a crown of thorns on his head defying the might of a whole empire. And if I raise resistances of a non-violent character I simply and humbly follow in the footsteps of the great teachers named by my critic.

Gandhi's Message

Edgar Snow

American journalist Edgar Snow interviewed Gandhi in 1928, a few days before Gandhi's assassination. In this article Snow claims that Gandhi is a national hero. According to Snow, Gandhi won national independence for more people than any other national leader. He spent his life teaching kindness and self-sacrifice and implemented a human rights crusade for 50 million untouchables. Snow evaluates Gandhi's lifelong quest for truth in all religions and the lessons of his political methods. Although tolerating the rich, Gandhi's mission was the downtrodden. Snow says that at the time of Gandhi's death, India's democracy had just begun. He believes that the social progress, truth, and equality for which Gandhi was martyred became not only his legacy but also the new responsibility of his followers.

Every Indian lost his father when Gandhi died. That is a plain fact, and it could never have been more so of any national hero. Yet here was something that meant more than that. This small man, so full of a large love of men, extended beyond India and beyond time. And he took the world into himself, or the part of it that felt his

Edgar Snow, "The Message of Gandhi," www.mkgandhi.org.

pull psychically or rationally or solely by the erosion of years, as in my own case. There was a mirror in the Mahatma in which everyone could see the best in himself, and when the mirror broke, it seemed that the thing in oneself might be fled forever. And that was what [Jawaharlal] Nehru meant when his first words that night were "The light has gone out of our lives.". . .

Gandhi won national independence for more millions of people than any other leader of men, and with less bloodshed, and that was the truth. He showed the weak and the poor how to struggle without taking life, and that was the truth. He spent years in jail for the national cause, and once he helped conduct the prosecution against himself after violence occurred in a civil-disobedience movement. He broke the system of indentured Indian labour in South Africa. He won respect for Indians and restored the self-respect of men who had humiliated them. He fought colour and racial discrimination everywhere. And all that was the truth. He laid the foundations for a national language which would bring men close together regardless of creed, and he nursed and tended the sick and the helpless to teach men kindliness and self-sacrifice. Against 3,000 years of prejudice he raised a crusade for the human rights of 50,000,000 untouchables, and he opposed the bigotry and dogmatism and the hateful orthodoxy of the caste system with more success than any Indian since Gautama Buddha.

The Quest for Truth
Gandhi never ceased to try to unite his countrymen and indeed the whole world under the homely injunctions common to all faiths: individual perfection, tolerance, humility, love of nature (God), equality, brotherhood and co-operation. He won a host of nonviolent battles for reform. Of course, he made mistakes and took false

turnings, and he was the first to impose suffering on himself when he wrongly advised others. But each of his efforts, including his last fast to prevent war, was for Gandhi some part of the truth or his endless quest for it. . . .

Gandhi's teachings are written in monumental volume, but here I am chiefly concerned with understanding his political method and the lessons it may have for us. I think it may be fairly summarised by saying that he became an *avatar* [an incarnation of a Hindu deity] for three reasons. He embodied man's need for meditation based on attainment of individual moral perfection, man's need for collective reform in social justice and equality, and man's need of an effective means to achieve

Mohandas Gandhi meets with Prime Minister Nehru of India (left) in 1946. Nehru helped Gandhi in his fight for international human rights.

individual and collective reform by nonviolent action.

We have had many teachers with answers to one or two of these needs, but Gandhi was the only man in our time who combined all three in his dynamic truth with highly positive results. Yet he was humble in his consciousness of failure. A few days before he was killed, he told me that he had lately become aware that "our fight for independence was not entirely one without war.". . .

Of the three needs or truths about modern man which Gandhi personified, it was the first—the attainment of inner purity—which was his hardest task. But it was the foundation of all his influence with the Indian people. When [Indian poet] Rabindranath Tagore first called him "the great soul" (*Mahatma*), it was in recognition of his attainment of *arya-dharma*, or "the religion of the noble soul." Gandhi was a puritan, but he was not a bigot. Thus, when I asked whether it was from Hindu, Muslim, Christian or other scriptures that he had first got his inspiration, he replied that the lesson was to be found in every great teaching, not just religious. The identity of truth with all other virtues had first struck him on reading the *Vedas*, but for him all truth was religion.

"There is no greater religion than truth," he quoted from Hindu scriptures.

One thing he could not abide was lying, and he knew a lie when he saw one, whether in the party press or from the pulpit of the church, and whether it was from an enemy or propaganda for a cause in which he believed.

"For me, means and ends are practically identical," he said. "We cannot attain right ends by way of falsehoods."

Gandhi thought he had to put that into practice internally as well as externally, and that he could not lead Indians to freedom until he had freed himself. He early decided that renunciation precedes certainty and precedes truth, and all his asceticism sprang from that tireless search—his preference for "innocent food," his rejection of wine and tobacco, his refusal to own anything, his *brahmacharya*, or self-restraint in sex, his many other abstentions.

"Thou hypocrite, cast out first the beam out of thine own eye, and then shalt thou see clearly to cast out the mote that is in thy brother's eye." He himself never claimed that he had cast out the beam and he never called himself the Mahatma. It was his fellow men who recognised it and elevated him to power and authority he never acknowledged.

In Gandhi's teachings and writings, I think you will find no lies, no meanness, no slander, no dogmatism, no hypocrisy, no fear, no arrogance, no false pride, no hatred, no claims of infallibility. His "inner voice"— and for him God was simply "an indefinable, mysterious power that pervades everything"—spoke gently always, and humbly, and it was the mirror in him which made bright the truth in other men and reflected and magnified it into a great light. He followed Buddha in employing the actions and arguments of love for dynamic ends.

"Speak the truth," Buddha said, "and let a man overcome anger by love; let him overcome the liar by truth."

Like Buddha, too, it was Gandhi's urge to liberate man which set him apart from the mass of mystics who seek only realisation of self in the anti-social practice of asceticism. Many people will misinterpret him as a mere saint or crazy idealist, and he has often been so lampooned in the West. But "politics divorced from religion have absolutely no meaning for me," he said, and he demonstrated that the epigram also applied in reverse. He was a practical social reformer and, in the true dialectical sense, a great revolutionary. For Gandhi in himself was the living synthesis of good means and good ends.

Misunderstood

Gandhi was often misunderstood, by myself among others, for his tolerance of the corrupt rich and powerful, and for his concessions to them. But on this visit to India he made me see clearly that he was always and everywhere with the oppressed and the downtrodden. Going back through his works, you won't find in retrospect that he ever compromised with wealth and power in either British or Indian hands, except for what he thought were the best interests of the people. One must comprehend Gandhi as a national leader who during most of his life served as the focus of infinitely varied and complex social forces which he had to unite for his main purpose. And once he had achieved national independence he began to throw the weight of his whole personality on the side of the progressive thesis of international reform and regeneration.

"Gandhi is always on the progressive side of things," India's Socialist leader, Jai Prakash Narain, told me only a few days before the murder. "Gandhi is our mightiest force against all the most backward elements in Indian society."

Like [German political philosopher Karl] Marx, Gandhi hated the state and wished to eliminate it, and he told me he considered himself "a philosophical anarchist." But he was a practical socialist in that he never opposed the state as a necessary instrument in achieving social democracy, though democracy as he understood it is certainly not to be confused with the kind of police state ruled by the Kremlin. . . .

Strictly speaking," Gandhi once said, "all amassing or hoarding of wealth above and beyond one's legitimate requirements is theft. There would be no occasion for theft, and therefore no thieves, if there were wise regulations of wealth and absolute social justice."

He wanted social ownership of large industry combined with a co-operative agrarian economy and small industrial co-operatives such as those in China that I had told him about. But he wanted the state to take over by peaceful means, and he "would not dispossess moneyed men by force, but would invite their co-operation in the process of conversion to state ownership. There are no pariahs in society. Whether they are millionaires or paupers, the two are sores of the same disease."

Gandhi said that he had "accepted the theory of socialism" even "while I was in South Africa thirty years ago. The basis of socialism is economic equality. There can be no rule of God in the present state of iniquitous inequalities in which a few roll in riches and the masses do not get enough to eat."

In a country where 20 percent of the population are always slowly starving, where another 40 percent get just barely enough to eat, and where there are at the same time some of the very wealthiest men in the world, Gandhi knew that a struggle for collective reform was imperative. In his last editorial in *Harijan*, he upbraided the Congress Party, which "but yesterday was the servant of the nation," but having "won political freedom, has yet to win economic freedom, social freedom and moral freedom."

Politics and Human Rights

He was under no delusions that India's emancipation had more than just begun. "The hardest tasks lie ahead," he said in the "difficult ascent to democracy." Ending on a note which for him was almost a thunderbolt of wrath, he declared, "Thank God [the Congress] is now no longer in sole possession of the field!" . . .

No one who spoke to him in his last days and who could follow his idiom at all can doubt that he was deeply dissatisfied with the corruption in government and the failure to extirpate the weedy communal groups which were sponsoring violence and the persecution of Muslims. That the influence of these groups had even permeated the government to some degree seemed clear when Gandhi launched his last fast in protest against failure to establish Hindu-Muslim amity.

Gandhi was on Nehru's side in the government—the liberal-democratic side which accepted his program of "social justice." And he repeatedly said that Jawaharlal was his political heir. Until his death, the right wing seemed to be winning out but it was "playing with fire," the Mahatma is said to have told one visitor. . . .

What remains to be revealed is whether the body of men and women who now shape the destiny of India can summon among themselves the collective discipline and the inner purity necessary to command the love and following which Gandhi's death left unclaimed, in order to impose the social progress and the promised justice and equality for which men believe the Mahatma died. The odds are overwhelmingly against it, yet no more than they were when Gandhi first began his fight against the mightiest empire in history.

It is a heavy responsibility to carry before the eyes of the world, the heritage of a saint who declared himself socialist. But if these children to whom he has now entrusted the nation may find new ways of synthesizing the needs of man, as he did in peaceful and vibrant brotherhood, the mirror may be rediscovered. Then the world may give India homage, and truth may yet rule before all men burn in the hatred and fanaticism that consumed the body of Gandhi, but not the great soul.

Profiles · in · History

Nelson Mandela: South African Activist

Commitment to Freedom

C. Stone Brown

C. Stone Brown introduces Nelson Mandela as a leader influenced from childhood to right the iniquities he saw endemic to black South Africans. Mandela and others formed a mass movement to reach blacks and encourage them to challenge the unjust apartheid system. Mandela also lobbied other countries for support and arranged for guerrilla warfare training to enable their cause. But what began as peaceful demonstrations turned violent, and Mandela was arrested. At the age of seventy-two, uncompromising in his support for democracy, the South African government buckled to international pressure, and Mandela walked out of prison a free man after twenty-seven years. Brown details Mandela's self-sacrificing journey to give his own life to the cause of freedom for all black South Africans. Brown is a regular contributor to *Crisis* magazine.

Many years ago, when I was a boy brought up in my village in the Transkei, I listened to the elders of the tribe telling stories about the good old days, before the arrival of the white man. Then, our people lived peacefully under the democratic rule of their kings and moved freely and confidently up and down the country without hindrance. Then the country was our own. We occupied the land, the forests, the rivers, we extracted the mineral wealth beneath the soil and all the riches of the beautiful land. I hoped and vowed then, that amongst the pleasures that life might offer me, would be the opportunity to serve my people and make my own humble contribution to their struggle for freedom.

—Nelson Rolihlahla Mandela

There are few men of good will in this world whose middle name means "making trouble." But that's the translation, from the Xhosa language, of the middle name of Nelson Rolihlahla Mandela, who made trouble for tyranny by making a "humble" contribution to the struggle of black South Africans and other freedom loving people around the world.

After decades of international protest, boycotts, economic sanctions, and mass killings of black South Africans, the defeat of apartheid would ultimately center on Mandela's freedom. Millions around the world applauded his release from prison by the South African government on February 11, 1990. It also signaled the end of apartheid and the country's transition to a democratically elected government.

African Americans have a special connection to Mandela. They seized upon his struggle as if it were their own. No one would disagree that the pressure from African Americans—who organized corporate and governmental boycotts of those investing or doing business in South Africa—helped lead to Mandela's release and the dismantling of apartheid. Yet for many African Americans, Mandela is an enigmatic figure, about whom little is known prior to his imprisonment.

Mandela's father was Chief Hendry Mgadla Mandela, the principal councilor to the acting paramount chief of Thembuland. Upon his father's death, young Nelson became the paramount's chief ward. The cases he saw provided him with first-hand knowledge of the iniquities endemic to black South Africa and greatly influenced his decision to become an attorney.

Mandela's introduction to political resistance came while at the University of Fort Hare, one of the few universities open to black Africans. He and other students were sent home for protesting the quality of the school's food. His guardian not only insisted that Mandela acquiesce to school authority, but also decided that it was time Mandela get married.

Being strong willed, Mandela refused to marry a hand-picked wife, indicative of a man who would later become celebrated for democratic principles. To escape the marriage, Mandela fled to Johannesburg.

For Mandela and black South Africans, Johannesburg represented what the northern United States represented for African Americans in the 1920's, a place of hope and opportunity. There he encountered relaxed segregation laws, people of diverse racial backgrounds who socialized and attended the same schools.

Although Johannesburg also offered an assortment of political organizations to join, Mandela settled on the African National Congress (ANC), an easy choice after meeting one of its leaders, Walter Sisulu, who took an immediate liking to the young Mandela. Sisulu and Mandela's relationship developed into one of student and teacher. Sisulu provided Mandela with a job, subsidized the continuation of his studies at Witwatersrand University and even purchased the suit Mandela wore at graduation in 1942. Mandela would soon become a central figure in the South Africa freedom movement.

The African National Congress was founded in 1912 by an elite group of middle-class black African men. Far from being the mass-movement it would become, the ANC was a pacifist organization, addressing concerns of the black middle class. Its strategy to change anti-black South African policies was based on humanitarian and moral grounds, principles that were foreign to the white South African government.

The ANC's pacifist philosophy remained intact until a brief fling in the 1920's with nationalist leanings under president Josiah Gumede. Influenced greatly by the panAfrican nationalist writings of Marcus Garvey, Gumede attempted to translate that appeal to the conditions of black South Africans. His detractors within the ranks of the ANC, however, rejected any form of militancy. Gumede's nationalist leanings would prevent his reelection as president in 1930. Gumede's legacy, however, would later engender debate over the organization's strategy.

While the ANC wrestled with its tactics and goals, the white ruling party of J.B. Hertzog was designing the legislative blueprint for the apartheid system in 1936. In 1948, the National Party won on an apartheid platform. The ANC responded by forming the African National Congress Youth League (ANCYL).

The ANCYL was composed of 60 young, vigorous, and radical-thinking members of the ANC. Notable names among them were Walter Sisulu, Oliver R. Tambo, Ashby P. Mda, and Nelson Mandela. The mission of the ANCYL was not to alienate the ANC base, but to broaden the ANC into a mass movement, reaching out to urban youth, the black working-class and peasants.

The ANCYL immediately instituted its "Programme of Action," a strategy that included boycotts, labor strikes, and civil disobedience. The Programme of Action represented a symbolic shift in previous ANC official policy. No longer would the young revolutionar-

ies be handcuffed by the conservative ideology of their elders.

Mandela immediately stood out among his ANCYL peers, demonstrating leadership, organizational skills and, most importantly, commitment to the struggle. In 1952, Mandela became president of the ANCYL, and president of the Transvaal region of the ANC. Given these responsibilities, Mandela devised the "M-Plan" or "Mandela Plan," a course of action to strengthen local and regional branches and hold covert meetings.

By 1953, the white government was tightening the yoke of oppression on black South Africans. For example, Sophiatown, a black neighborhood of Johannesburg where blacks could own property, was forcibly turned over to white South Africans. The Bantustan policy would soon follow, assigning blacks to territories called "homelands." Black education was limited to service-sector jobs. The "pass laws" required black South Africans to have a "pass" to obtain work, travel or be out after curfew.

In 1956, the government arrested Mandela and 155 others, charging them with treason. The courts, however, would eventually rule in favor of the defendants. During the trial, Mandela would meet his future wife Winnie Nomzamo Madikizela. Their marriage would last 30 years, only three of them together.

Mandela Goes Underground

What began as a peaceful demonstration to protest the pass laws in the town of Sharpeville resulted in 69 dead and over 200 injuries, most shot in the back. Another protest near Cape Town resulted in two dead and 49 injured. The government imposed a state of emergency and outlawed all anti-government organizations.

With the ANC banned, Mandela was forced underground. Over time, Mandela would lose contact with his family and the law practice he built with Walter Sisulu. Even during this period, Mandela showed no signs of wavering in his commitment to the struggle for freedom.

To continue moving about the country undetected, Mandela often disguised himself as a laborer or chauffeur. By 1961, the government's policies required the ANCYL to change its strategy. This led to the formation of a specialized armed unit of the ANC, "Umkhonto we Sizwe" or MK Policy, with Mandela as the commander-in-chief.

Mandela would later explain why the MK Policy was instituted:

> At the beginning of June 1961, after long and anxious assessment of the South African situation, I and some colleagues came to the conclusion that as vio-

lence in this country was inevitable, it would be wrong and unrealistic for African leaders to continue preaching peace and non-violence at a time when the government met our peaceful demands with force. It was only when all else failed, when all channels of peaceful protest had been barred to us, that the decision was made to embark on violent forms of political struggle, and to form the Umkhonto we Sizwe. The government had left us no other choice.

ANC members had virtually no military training or access to munitions. To tackle these problems, Mandela left the country to lobby for support: "In January 1962, I toured Africa, visiting Tanganyika, Ethiopia, Libya, Tunisia, Algeria, Morocco, Mali, Senegal, Guinea, Sierra Leone, Liberia, Ghana and Nigeria. I also visited England. In all these countries I met the heads of state or other senior government officials."

Mandela also arranged for guerrilla warfare training for the MK Policy. Mandela's tour would go a long way in advancing the ANC's cause, but he would eventually pay a hefty price.

Arrested, Tried, Convicted

On August 5, 1962, Mandela was arrested and charged with two counts: Illegally leaving the country without authorization, and assisting in organizing the illegal strike of May 1961. Mandela, a trained attorney, chose to defend himself, arguing that he wasn't only defending himself but the fights and aspirations of all black South Africans.

Mandela petitioned the court to drop all charges, on the basis that all who would sit in judgment of him were white: "I consider myself neither legally nor morally bound to obey laws made by a parliament in which I have no representation. In a political trial such as this one, which involves a clash of the aspirations of the African people and those of whites, the country's courts, as presently constituted, cannot be impartial and fair."

As reasonable as Mandela's argument resonated, the case echoed the ruling handed down in America's infamous Dred Scott decision of 1857. Mandela effectively had no rights. The court rejected his argument and found him guilty of all charges, sentencing him to five years in prison.

While Mandela was serving his five-year sentence, several ANC members, who continued their underground operations, were charged with sabotage, treason, and violent conspiracy. Mandela, already serving five years, was also charged in the case. This time, Mandela would be sentenced to life in prison. At the time of sentencing, Mandela eloquently reminded his oppressors of his resilience:

> I have fought against white domination, and I have fought against black domination. I have cherished the ideal of a democratic and free society in which all persons live together in harmony and with equal opportunities. It is an ideal for which I hope to live for and to achieve. But if need be, it is an ideal for which I'm prepared to die.

That statement has become a classic declaration of freedom and political resistance.

Long Walk to Freedom

Mandela would spend the next 18 years of his life at the notorious Robben Island maximum-security prison. While the inhumane conditions would have broken an ordinary man, Mandela and his co-conspirators incredulously continued their efforts from prison to liberate black South Africans from apartheid. Mandela also secretly wrote and smuggled-out his autobiography, *Long Walk to Freedom*.

Mandela had every opportunity to shorten his long walk to freedom. While serving his life sentence, he often turned down government offers of freedom in exchange for accepting apartheid policies. He all but laughed at authorities when, in the 1980's at the height of impassioned black student protest, he was offered his freedom on the condition that he renounce violence.

"Prisoners cannot enter into contracts," he pointedly reasoned. "Only free men can negotiate."

Mandela would be released on February 11, 1990, but not under compromising conditions. In fact, it would be the South African government which would eventually buckle to domestic and international pressure to end apartheid policies.

The transition to a new constitution and democratic government would not be a smooth undertaking. As one might expect, the far-right radical whites resisted to yield their power to a black majority rule. But with Mandela and President [F.W.] de Klerk committed to a democratic constitution, the far-right would eventually surrender.

In 1993, Mandela won the Nobel Peace prize. In 1994, he became South Africa's first democratically elected president. He retired from public life in 1999, and currently resides in Qunu Transkei.

Nelson Rolihlahla Mandela is a rare man because he was willing to sacrifice his own life so that others could be free. He was 72 years old when he was released from prison, but he never compromised his position.

Now, no longer will the elders have to tell stories to the young about the "good old days before the arrival of the white man." The stories now are of Mandela, Sisulu, Tambo and others who, through courageous determination, transformed South Africa into a democratic nation.

How Prison Influenced Mandela's Commitment to Human Rights

John Battersby

In an interview with John Battersby with the *Christian Science Monitor*, Nelson Mandela, the former president of South Africa, discusses how his twenty-seven years in prison contributed to his personal development and influenced the life he lives today.

Mandela says one of the most difficult things to change is oneself. He credits prison for teaching him to reflect, respect all people, and follow a highly disciplined regime that influenced his behavior and thinking. On reflection, Mandela says the single biggest threat to society is poverty; those who recognize this and think about the poor are the world's real leaders. Battersby interviewed Mandela to record the experiences and philosophies that helped make Mandela one of the heroes of the twentieth century.

John Battersby, "Mandela," *Christian Science Monitor*, vol. 92, February 10, 2000, p. 15. Copyright © 2000 by The Christian Science Publishing Society. All rights reserved. Reproduced by permission.

Despite his reluctance to be singled out and discuss his personal qualities, there is consensus in South Africa that without Mandela's personal commitment to reconciliation, his moral authority, integrity, and intense compassion, the country's transition to democracy might not have gone as smoothly.

Mandela is at pains to ensure that he is remembered as an ordinary mortal with qualities that are within the reach of ordinary people. "What always worried me in prison was [that I could acquire] the image of someone who is always 100 percent correct and can never do any wrong," he told one audience of 500. "People expect me to perform far beyond my ability."

He expanded on these reflections for the first time in a recent interview with the [*Christian Science*] *Monitor*, which probed his philosophy of reconciliation, the origins of his moral integrity, and the experiences and influences that forged the qualities which have made him one of the heroes of the 20th century.

He also spoke about the importance of religion in his life and the crucial role of reflection and "the time to think" during his 27 years in jail.

History will remember Mandela for having the strength of conviction to risk engaging his jailers—and thereby humanizing them—from inside prison and eventually setting the stage for the ANC to negotiate them out of power. Mandela sees the success of the ANC in mobilizing both domestic and international opinion against the apartheid government as the key factor.

In the interview, Mandela insisted that he wanted to be remembered as part of a collective and not in isolation. On his release from jail [in 1990], he made it clear that he regarded himself as a "loyal and obedient servant" of the African National Congress (ANC), the liberation movement he headed before becoming South Africa's first democratically elected president in May 1994.

"I would like to be remembered as part of a team, and I would like my contribution to be assessed as somebody who carried out decisions taken by that collective," Mandela says, adding that even if he wanted to be remembered in a specific way that was not a realistic option.

Mandela was speaking in the living room of the house he shares with his second wife Graca Machel, whom he married in 1998. It is a double-story house in the plush Johannesburg neighborhood of Houghton.

"As prisoners, we used our individual and collective positions to make friends with some of our jailers. But this must be understood against the bigger picture of what was happening outside—an organized and disciplined struggle by our organization and the international community," he says.

No Sainthood

At the launch, late [in 1999], of a book to commemorate him, written by South African journalist Charlene Smith, Mandela insisted that he not be elevated to some kind of sainthood.

The paradoxical side of the man is that he has sometimes taken on superhuman tasks such as his shuttle last October [1999] to Iran, Syria, Jordan, Israel, Gaza, and the United States in a bid to broker a comprehensive Middle East peace.

Despite what Mandela described as "positive and cordial" meetings with Israeli Prime Minister Ehud Barak and President Ezer Weizman, Israel rejected his intervention. But Mandela was not unduly discouraged.

"There are bound to be setbacks," he says.

Mandela was greatly encouraged by the eventual outcomes of his interventions in East Timor and the handing over by Libya of those accused of the bombing of the Pan Am flight over the Scottish town of Lockerbie in 1988. He spent seven years mediating the behind-the-scenes negotiations with Saudi Arabia.

He says it is important that leaders should be presented to people with their weaknesses and all. "If you come across as a saint, people can become very discouraged," he says. "I was once a young man and I did all the things young men do," Mandela says, to drive home the point of his human fallibility.

Biographers and commentators have been intrigued by Mandela's extraordinary focus and unity of purpose during his years as a young ANC activist and later as its spiritual leader from behind bars.

"If you have an objective in life, then you want to concentrate on that and not engage in infighting with your enemies," he says in the interview, "You want to create an atmosphere where you can move everybody towards the goal you have set for yourself—as well as the collective for which you work.

"And, therefore, for all people who have found themselves in the position of being in jail and trying to transform society, forgiveness is natural because you have no time to be retaliative. . . . You want to mobilize everybody to support your cause and the aims you have set for your life," he says.

Asked about the origins of his passionate belief in reconciliation and forgiveness, Mandela goes into a lengthy explanation of how he launched the Mandela Children's Fund after a personal encounter with homeless children in Cape Town who had come to see him to explain their plight. He was so moved that he vowed in that moment to launch the fund, which has collected more than $25 million and has helped hundreds of children. Mandela donated a third of his presidential salary to the fund during his five years in office. Many business executives matched his example and some bettered it.

What Price Reconciliation?

Mandela is sensitive to criticism from certain black leaders that he has leaned over too far toward whites in his efforts to achieve reconciliation and forgiveness. He becomes emotional when defending his impressive campaign over the past few years to get business leaders to donate funds for the building of schools and clinics in the rural areas.

"Why would anyone say that I am leaning too much towards whites? Tell me the record of any black man in this country who has done as much as that [for black people]. . . . I am not aware of any other black man who has spent so much time addressing the problems of poverty, lack of education, and disease amongst our people," Mandela says, adding that he had nothing but cooperation and support from the white business community.

When it comes to his moral authority and achievement in persuading his jailers and their political bosses to negotiate with him, Mandela again stresses the moral high ground of the ANC cause.

"When you have attained the moral high ground, it is better to confront your people directly and say: Let's sit down and talk. So, it is not something that just comes from me. It is something that was worked out by the organization to which I belong."

Mandela speaks of the influence that veteran ANC leader Walter Sisulu had had on him while in prison and how he was instrumental in taking care of fellow prisoners regardless of their political background.

Mandela has in turn been praised by Eddie Daniels, a former Robben Island prisoner from a rival anti-apartheid organization, who has told how Mandela befriended him and kept his cell clean when he was ill.

Mandela says, "I can tell you that a man like Sisulu was almost like a saint in things of that nature.

"You would really admire him because he is continually thinking about other people.

"I learned a great deal from him—not only on that respect but also, politically, he was our mentor. He is a very good fellow . . . and humble. He led from behind and put others in front, but he reversed the position in situations of danger. Then he chose to be in the front line."

In *Mandela: The Authorized Biography* (Knopf), Anthony Sampson notes the remarkable transformation in the Mandela that emerged from jail compared with the impulsive activist with a quick temper he knew in the late 1950s.

Mandela does not dispute Mr. Sampson's judgment and acknowledges the importance of mastering his anger while in prison. "One was angry at what was happening [in apartheid South Africa]—the humiliation, the loss of our human dignity. We tended to react in accordance with anger and our emotion rather than sitting down and thinking about things properly.

"But in jail—especially for those who stayed in single cells—you had enough opportunity to sit down and think. And you were in contact with a lot of people who had a high education and who were widely traveled. When they told of their experiences, you felt humbled.

"All those influences changed one," Mandela says. Sampson quotes from a letter that Mandela wrote to his then wife, Winnie, in 1981 after she had been jailed.

Mandela noted that there were qualities "in each one of us" that form the basis of our spiritual life and that we can change ourselves by observing our reactions to the unfolding of life.

He urged Winnie in the letter "to learn to know yourself . . . to search realistically and regularly the processes of your own mind and feelings."

In the interview, Mandela says that one of the most powerful forces that changed him was thinking about how he had behaved and reacted to generosity and compassion expressed toward him in the past.

"For example, when I arrived in Johannesburg [as a young man], I was poor, and many people helped me get by. But when I became a lawyer and I was in a better position [financially], I became too busy with legal affairs and forgot about people who had helped me.

"Instead of going to them and saying: Look, here's a bunch of flowers or a box of chocolates and saying thank you, I had never even thought about these things. I felt that I had behaved like a wild man . . . like an animal and I really criticized myself for the way I had behaved.

"But I was able to do this because I had time to think about it, whereas outside jail—from morning to sunset—you are moving from one meeting to the other, and there is no time to think about problems. Thinking is one of the most important weapons in dealing with problems . . . and we didn't have that outside."

Peter Ustinov, the veteran actor, author, and international citizen, met Mandela in South Africa two years ago and was struck by the importance Mandela attached to the long period of solitude in prison.

"I had a most inspiring meeting with Nelson Mandela," Ustinov told this reporter in an interview in the Swiss Alpine town of Davos. "He told me with a certain amount of irony and wickedness: 'I am grateful for the 27 years I spent in prison because it gave me the opportunity to meditate and think deeply. . . . But since I came out of prison, I haven't had the time.'"

Time for Reflection

How has Mandela made time to think since his release from jail in 1990? He says that he has tried to emulate the practice of businessmen who take a complete break from their work over weekends. Mandela says he consciously has tried to make time for reflection.

After his separation from Winnie, Mandela used to spend long periods in retreat in the home of a wealthy Afrikaner businessman, Douw Steyn, who ran an open house for the ANC to hold meetings during the negotiations with the government. It was here that Mandela proofread the script of his autobiography: *Long Walk to Freedom* (Little Brown).

In November last year, Mandela accepted an invitation to be the guest speaker at a gala evening to mark the transformation of the house into a super-luxury guest house, retreat, and conference center.

In an impromptu speech, Mandela waxed philosophical and introspective in paying tribute to the warmth and hospitality of his Afrikaner hosts.

"It has been said that difficulties and disaster destroy some people and make others," Mandela began. It was a phrase he had last used in a letter to Winnie in 1975. "Douw Steyn is one of those who has turned disaster into success," he said of the wealthy businessman who had formerly supported apartheid.

Change Yourself

"One of the most difficult things is not to change society—but to change yourself," he said. "I came to stay here at some of the most difficult moments, and the way Liz and Douw treated me has left me with fond memories."

Mandela said that Douw Steyn had changed and was now part of the white business community that was sharing its resources with the poor. That gave him a feeling of fulfillment.

"It enables me to go to bed with an enriching feeling in my soul and the belief that I am changing myself [by reconciling with former adversaries]," Mandela said. . . .

Mandela said that religion had played a very important role in his life. He has tended to avoid talking about the subject in the past.

In December [1999], Mandela addressed a gathering of religious leaders from the world's major faiths in Cape Town. He spoke publicly about his views on religion for the first time.

"I appreciate the importance of religion. You have to have been in a South African jail under apartheid where you could see the cruelty of human beings to each other in its naked form. Again, religious institutions and their leaders gave us hope that one day we would return."

Mandela said that real leaders were those who thought about the poor 24 hours a day and who knew in their hearts that poverty was the single biggest threat to society.

"We have sufficient cause to be cynical about humanity. We have seen enough injustice, strife, division, suffering, and pain, and our capacity to be massively inhuman. But this gathering counters despairing cynicism and reaffirms the nobility of the human spirit," Mandela said.

The Power of Religion

Mandela went on to say, "Religion is one of the most important forces in the world. Whether you are a Christian, a Muslim, a Buddhist, a Jew, or a Hindu, religion is a great force, and it can help one have command of one's own morality, one's own behavior, and one's own attitude."

"Religion has had a tremendous influence on my own life. You must remember that during our time—right from Grade 1 up to university—our education was provided by religious institutions. I was in [Christian] missionary schools. The government [of the day] had no interest whatsoever in our education and, therefore, religion became a force which was responsible for our development," he said.

The discipline of jail also played a role in his transformation, he said.

"It was difficult, of course, to always be disciplined before one went to jail except to say that I have always liked sport. And to that extent I was disciplined in the sense that four days a week I went to the gym for at least two hours.

"Also, I was a lawyer, and I had to be disciplined to keep up with events in the legal field, and to that extent I was disciplined," he said.

But Mandela said there were many respects in which he and his colleagues were not disciplined when they went to jail.

"In prison, you had to follow a highly disciplined regime, and that, of course, influenced your behavior and your thinking," he said.

Mandela said there was also a personal discipline. "We continued to do our own exercises, and we continued with study and conversing with others to gain from their experiences."

He said that reading the biographies of the great leaders of the century also had a major impact on him. Mandela said it was through reading the biographies that he realized that problems make some people and destroy others. Mandela said that the prison experience taught him to respect even the most ordinary people. "I have been surprised a great deal sometimes when I see somebody who looks less than ordinary, but when you talk to the person and he (or she) opens his mouth, he is something completely different.

"It is possible that if I had not gone to jail and been able to read and to listen to the stories of many people . . . I might not have learned these things."

Ending Apartheid

James Ryan

Nelson Mandela spent twenty-seven years in prison for opposing the apartheid political system that sanctioned legal segregation of and discrimination against black South Africans. When political pressure forced his jailers to release him from prison, Mandela was considered a silent, suffering martyr. He became the head of the African National Congress and continued to work to end apartheid. He was elected South Africa's first black president in 1994. As president, he continued to restore human rights to the people, stimulate foreign investment to grow the economy, and return land taken from black South Africans during the previously unjust apartheid system.

James Ryan presents a biography of this South African statesman who spent his entire life furthering the human rights of his countrymen.

🐒 🐒 🐒

Rolihlahla Dalibhunga Mandela was born on July 18, 1918 in the village of Qunu, in the Transkei, South Africa. His father was a chief of the Thembu tribe and a trusted counselor to the Thembuland royal family, and he hoped that one day his son would take his right-

James Ryan, "Ending Apartheid," *Political and World Leaders: Post–Cold War*, 2002, p. 124. Copyright © 2002 by Great Neck Publishing. Reproduced by permission.

ful place as a tribal leader. However, his father died when Mandela was nine years old, and the boy became a ward of the tribe's acting regent.

Mandela was given the English name "Nelson" on his first day at Healdtown Methodist Boarding School. Later, he attended Fort Hare University for two years, before being expelled in 1940 for participating in a student demonstration. After completing his undergraduate degree via correspondence, Mandela enrolled in Witwatersrand University to study law, and obtained a position with a law firm in Johannesburg.

Opposing Apartheid

In 1944, Mandela became active in the African National Congress (ANC), a political party dedicated to securing civil rights for all non-white South Africans. Although the ANC adhered to the principles of nonviolence, many younger nationalists were disillusioned with the party's apparent lack of progress. These tensions came to a head with the election of the National Party, led by Daniel Malan, in 1948. Malan first instituted the infamous system of apartheid ("apartness"), which sanctioned legal segregation and discrimination against black South Africans.

Mandela believed, along with many of his peers, that nonviolent protests against apartheid served only to instigate police brutality. He joined the ANC Youth League (ANCYL), which had been formed by the more militant members of the ANC. The ANCYL's 1949 Program of Action called for widespread boycotts and strikes. When Mandela was elected national president of the Youth League in 1951, he quickly launched the Defiance Campaign, designed to organize a large-scale resistance movement and work toward the repeal of discriminatory legislation.

In 1952, Mandela was arrested under the Suppression

of Communism Act. Although his sentence was suspended, he was banned from attending public gatherings, including ANC meetings, for several years. In addition to his work as a political activist, he opened a new law practice specializing in the defense of those being persecuted under apartheid. Mandela, along with other leaders of the resistance movement, was charged with treason in 1956. The case against them was eventually dropped, but court appearances and legal entanglements occupied most of Mandela's time during this period.

Mandela married social worker Winnie Madikizela in 1958. The couple would go on to have two daugh-

Long Walk to Freedom

Nelson Mandela describes his personal mission to make freedom a lifestyle for all the people in South Africa.

My commitment . . . to the millions of South Africans I would never know or meet, was at the expense of the people I knew best and loved most. It was as simple and yet as incomprehensible as the moment a small child asks her father, "Why can you not be with us?" And the father must utter the terrible words: "There are other children like you, a great many of them . . ." and then one's voice trails off. . . .

It was this desire for the freedom of my people to live their lives with dignity and self-respect that animated my life, that transformed a frightened young man into a bold one, that drove a law-abiding attorney to become a criminal, that turned a family-loving husband into a man without a home, that forced a life-loving man to live like a monk. I am no more virtuous or self-sacrificing than the next man, but I found that I could not even enjoy the poor and limited freedoms I was allowed when I knew my people were not free. Freedom is indivisible; the chains

ters together, Zenani and Zindzi. While he was busy dealing with the treason charges, Mandela's new wife took a more active role in the politics of the ANC.

The Spear of the Nation

On March 21, 1960, a group of anti-apartheid activists gathered in Sharpeville, near Johannesburg, to protest the passage of new laws restricting the movements of blacks within South Africa. Police opened fire on the demonstration, and killed 69 people. The national emergency that followed what came to be known as the Sharpeville Massacre resulted in a ban on the ANC,

on any one of my people were the chains on all of them, the chains on all of my people were the chains on me.

It was during those long and lonely years that my hunger for the freedom of my own people became a hunger for the freedom of all people, white and black. I knew as well as I knew anything that the oppressor must be liberated just as surely as the oppressed. A man who takes away another man's freedom is a prisoner of hatred, he is locked behind the bars of prejudice and narrow-mindedness. I am not truly free if I am taking away someone else's freedom, just as surely as I am not free when my freedom is taken from me. The oppressed and the oppressor alike are robbed of their humanity.

When I walked out of prison, that was my mission, to liberate the oppressed and the oppressor both. Some say that has now been achieved. But I know that that is not the case. The truth is that we are not yet free; we have merely achieved the freedom to be free, the right not to be oppressed. We have not taken the final step of our journey, but the first step on a longer and even more difficult road.

Nelson Mandela, *Long Walk to Freedom*. Boston: Little, Brown, 1994, pp. 543–44.

and the arrest of many of its leaders. Realizing that nonviolent protest against apartheid was futile, the ANC decided to adopt a policy of armed resistance.

In response to the ANC ban, the underground group Umkhonto we Sizwe (MK), "The Spear of the Nation," was formed by Mandela and other nationalist leaders in 1961. They used sabotage as a method of resistance, striking only government targets and other official symbols of apartheid. Mandela traveled throughout Africa and Europe to rally support for MK's cause, and to study guerilla warfare tactics.

When he returned to South Africa in 1962, Mandela was arrested for leaving the country illegally, as well as for his activities with MK. He was sentenced to five years in prison on Robben Island. While serving his sentence, Mandela was charged with high treason, and stood trial with the leaders of MK in the 1963–64 Rivonia Trial. During the trial, Mandela outlined the aims of Umkhonto we Sizwe, and reaffirmed his unwavering opposition to apartheid. Although they were spared execution, Mandela and his co-defendants were sentenced to life in prison.

Mandela returned to Robben Island in 1964 to begin serving his life sentence. Outside the prison, the resistance movement was as strong as ever. While public discussion of Mandela was outlawed, the black South African majority viewed him as a silent, suffering martyr. Fearing that his influence on his fellow prisoners was dangerous, the government had Mandela moved to a maximum-security facility in 1982, where he spent most of his time in solitary confinement. His wife, meanwhile, faced repeated imprisonment and harassment because of her support for her husband, and as a result, Winnie Mandela became more aggressive in her political opposition to apartheid.

Beginning in 1984, the South African government

began negotiations for Mandela's release, on the condition that he endorse a controversial plan to segregate blacks into designated "homelands." He refused the offers, and as civil disobedience and political violence escalated, many foreign governments began to sever diplomatic and economic ties with South Africa.

In 1988, Mandela was diagnosed with tuberculosis, and was subsequently moved to a less rigorous prison environment. As international support for the plight of Mandela and black South Africans continued to mount, the National Party had no choice but to respond to the pressure. By 1990, president of South Africa and head of the National Party F.W. de Klerk had revoked most of the apartheid laws, released many of the prisoners convicted in the Rivonia Trial, and lifted the restrictions imposed on the ANC. On February 11, 1990, following a series of negotiations with de Klerk, Mandela was finally given his freedom after spending twenty-seven years in prison.

Freedom

Upon his release, Mandela immediately started to rally support and raise funds for the South African civil rights movement. In 1991, Mandela was made president of the ANC, and he and de Klerk opened negotiations for the establishment of a democratic government. The two were awarded the Nobel Peace Prize in 1993.

South Africa held its first-ever free elections, open to all citizens, on April 27, 1994. The ANC received the majority of the popular vote, and Mandela was elected president. In order to make the transition to a democracy more representative of the South African majority, he formed a coalition cabinet with members from various ethnic groups. The new government established the Truth and Reconciliation Commission, which offered amnesty to those who had committed criminal acts under apartheid. Mandela also worked toward returning land seized from black South Africans during the era of apartheid, and encouraged foreign investment in order to stimulate the country's economy.

Mandela divorced his wife Winnie, who had been widely criticized for her endorsement of civil violence, in 1996. Two years later, on his eightieth birthday, he married Graca Machel. Although the sweeping reforms that he instituted were mostly successful, Mandela stepped down as president of South Africa in June 1999, choosing not to run against his vice president, Thabo Mbeki, who went on to win the presidential election that year.

Since retiring from the presidency, Mandela has acted as a mediator in several international disputes, and remains a vocal supporter of human rights. He was diagnosed with prostate cancer in 2001, and is undergoing treatment for the condition, which is not life-threatening.

Human Rights Progress

Nelson Mandela

South African president Nelson Mandela argues that fundamental human rights are still unavailable to many people around the world. Mandela contends that poverty, hunger, and the need for democratic rights enabling people to participate and determine their own destinies are goals that remain unattained. Mandela says happiness, justice, human dignity, peace, and prosperity were all part of the intent of the original Universal Declaration of Human Rights. In this speech delivered to the United Nations, Mandela challenges leaders to ensure world consistency in human rights.

❦ ❦ ❦

Quite appropriately, this 53rd General Assembly will be remembered through the ages as the moment at which we marked and celebrated the 50th Anniversary of the adoption of the Universal Declaration of Human Rights. Born in the aftermath of the defeat of the Nazi and fascist crime against humanity, this Declaration held high hope that all our societies would, in future, be

Nelson Mandela, address to the 53rd General Assembly of the United Nations, New York, September 21, 1998.

built on the foundation of the glorious vision spelt out in each of its clauses.

For those who had to fight for their emancipation, such as ourselves who, with your help, had to free ourselves from the criminal apartheid system, the Universal Declaration of Human Rights served as the vindication of the justice of our cause.

At the same time, it constituted a challenge to us that our freedom, once achieved, should be dedicated to the implementation of the perspectives contained in the Declaration.

Today, we celebrate the fact that this historic document has survived a turbulent five decades, which have seen some of the most extraordinary developments in the evolution of human society.

These include the collapse of the colonial system, the passing of a bipolar world, breath-taking advances in science and technology and the entrenchment of the complex process of globalisation.

And yet, at the end of it all, the human beings who are the subject of the Universal Declaration of Human Rights continue to be afflicted by wars and violent conflicts.

They have, as yet, not attained their freedom from fear and death that would be brought about by the use of weapons of mass destruction as well as conventional arms.

Many are still unable to exercise the fundamental and inalienable democratic rights that would enable them to participate in the determination of the destiny of their countries, nations, families and children and to protect themselves from tyranny and dictatorship.

The very right to be human is denied everyday to hundreds of millions of people as a result of poverty, the unavailability of basic necessities such as food, jobs, water and shelter, education, health care and a healthy environment.

The failure to achieve this vision contained in the Universal Declaration of Human Rights finds dramatic expression in the contrast between wealth and poverty which characterises the divide between the countries of the North and the countries of the South and within individual countries in all hemispheres. It is made especially poignant and challenging by the fact that this co-existence of wealth and poverty, the perpetuation of the practice of the resolution of inter and intra-state conflicts by war and the denial of the democratic right of many across the world, all result from the acts of com-

Nelson Mandela, leader of the African National Congress, speaks at a 1994 Cape Town rally. Mandela challenged UN world leaders to ensure human rights.

mission and omission particularly by those who occupy positions of leadership in politics, in the economy and in other spheres of human activity.

What I am trying to say is that all these social ills which constitute an offence against the Universal Declaration of Human Rights are not a pre-ordained result of the forces of nature or the product of a curse of the deities.

They are the consequences of decisions which men and women take or refuse to take, all of whom will not hesitate to pledge their devoted support for the vision conveyed in the Universal Declaration of Human Rights.

This Declaration was proclaimed as Universal precisely because the founders of this Organisation and the nations of the world who joined hands to fight the scourge of fascism, including many who still had to achieve their own emancipation, understood this clearly that our human world was an interdependent whole.

Necessarily, the values of happiness, justice, human dignity, peace and prosperity have a universal application because each people and every individual is entitled to them.

Similarly, no people can truly say it is blessed with happiness, peace and prosperity where others, as human as itself, continue to be afflicted with misery, armed conflict and terrorism and deprivation.

Thus can we say that the challenge posed by the next 50 years of the Universal Declaration of Human Rights, by the next century whose character it must help fashion, consists in whether humanity, and especially those who will occupy positions of leadership, will have the courage to ensure that, at last, we build a world consistent with the provisions of that historic Declaration and other human rights instruments that have been adopted since 1948.

3

Profiles · in · History

Freedom Fighters

Frederick Douglass: From Slave to Activist

Richard Conniff

After his escape from slavery at twenty, Frederick Douglass became the antislavery movement's voice of firsthand experience. Richard Conniff, author of the following viewpoint for *Smithsonian*, says it was Douglass's tireless efforts that helped lay the groundwork for the emancipation of slaves after the Civil War.

Conniff gives a glimpse into Douglass's life from his childhood as a house slave to his struggle to become a free man and establish himself as a fearless enemy of slave owners and "hypocrites." Douglass's speeches and writings advocated achieving freedom through the political system rather than violent rebellion. Douglass claimed that emancipation was morally right, and because of his focus on the issue of blacks as humans, he became the conscience of the Civil War effort. After President Abraham Lincoln issued the Emancipation Proclamation freeing slaves, Douglass fought for fundamental human rights and equality. Conniff is a journalist, essayist, and author of several books.

❧ ❧ ❧

Richard Conniff, "Frederick Douglass Always Knew He Was Meant to Be Free," *Smithsonian*, vol. 24, February 1995, p. 114. Copyright © 1995 by the *Smithsonian*. Reproduced by permission of the author.

Taking to the podium throughout his life, the former slave fought with tireless eloquence to 'secure the Blessings of Liberty' for all.

The "uproarious and happy boy" then known as Frederick Bailey was 6 years old on the morning his grandmother Betsey took his hand and walked him 12 miles into his life as a slave. It was a bright August day on the Eastern Shore of Maryland, hot and humid, he later wrote. At times, his grandmother had to tote him on her shoulders; at times, he walked beside her, imitating her practiced stride. When the dirt road took them into the woods, he clutched her hand at the sight of monstrous, staring figures, which turned out to be tree stumps.

Real terrors lay ahead that day in 1824, but about them his grandmother maintained "the reserve and solemnity of a priestess." She had been through these forced separations too many times before: like the other grandchildren she reared, Frederick had been someone else's property since birth, hers only on loan. In mid-afternoon they arrived at the Chesapeake Bay plantation where "old master" lived, and she set Frederick among the other slave children. Then, not wanting to prolong the sorrow of parting, she slipped away from him without a word. The boy wept himself to sleep that night, torn from "the only home I ever had." It was "my first introduction to the realities of slavery."

By the standards of slavery, Frederick was often to get favored treatment over the next 14 years. But the realities were to include hunger so sharp that he had to vie with the dog for table scraps, and cold so intense that his bare, calloused feet cracked open. Like other slaves, he was systematically denied family, education, even the knowledge of his own birth date. He saw his fellow slaves savagely beaten. He suffered the pencil-thick scars of the whip on his own back. These realities of slavery were an outrage Frederick refused to accept almost from that first day, and the struggle begun then would in time anger and inspire millions of Americans.

He called himself Frederick Douglass after he escaped to freedom at the age of 20, and he soon established himself in the antislavery movement as a fearless enemy of the slave owner and the hypocrite.

"What, to the American slave, is your Fourth of July?" he asked, in one impassioned speech, at a time when more than three million African-Americans remained in bondage. "To him, your celebration is a sham . . . your shouts of liberty and equality, hollow mockery. . . . There is not a nation on the Earth guilty of practices more shocking and bloody than are the people of the United States at this very hour."

White Americans came to his talks by the thousands, sometimes just to gawk or jeer. But they also listened, if only because Douglass shrewdly cast himself in a classic American mold, as an almost miraculously self-made man. To audiences in the decades before the Civil War, it was as if this slave—deemed a "chattel" by law—had leapt to the speaker's podium straight from his grandmother's cabin at Tuckahoe Creek. "It could speak," Douglass remarked mordantly. In truth, he spoke with wit, erudition and richness of voice to rival Daniel Webster's.

His physical presence was also commanding. He was more than six feet tall, with olive brown skin, a shock of hair slanting across his broad forehead, and flashing, wounded eyes. The feminist Elizabeth Cady Stanton vividly remembered the first time she heard Douglass speak, at an antislavery meeting in Boston, where he swept his listeners from laughter to tears on the tide of his voice. "All the other speakers seemed tame after Frederick Douglass," Stanton wrote. "He stood there like an African prince, majestic in his wrath.". . .

It was an astonishing life. "I feel greatly embarrassed when I attempt to address an audience of white people . . . it makes me tremble," he declared to a group of Massachusetts abolitionists in one of his earliest speeches. But it didn't stop him from adding: "Prejudice against color is stronger North than South; it hangs around my neck like a heavy weight."

Before there was a civil rights movement, before the word "racism" itself existed, Douglass led the movement that desegregated the schools of Rochester, New York, where he and his wife raised their family. Long before Rosa Parks refused to give up her seat to a white man on a segregated bus in Alabama, Douglass had to be dragged bodily from a whites-only railroad car in Massachusetts—and he tore the seat out with him. Before the assassinations of Malcolm X and Martin Luther King Jr., Douglass was repeatedly attacked and beaten by mobs yelling "Kill the damned nigger!" Repeatedly he fought back, and lived.

Nor did the pressing issues of race prevent him from advocating human liberty at large. At the Seneca Falls, New York, convention of 1848, where the feminist movement was born, Frederick Douglass was the only man to vote for women's suffrage. The newspaper he had founded the previous year proudly declared, "Right is of no sex, truth is of no color."

In time, the tireless voice of Frederick Douglass would help lay the groundwork for the emancipation of slaves in the Civil War and for the 15th Amendment to the Constitution, which, on paper, guaranteed black men the right to vote. But he would also live to see the failure of his grand vision that freedom and the vote would win blacks an equal place with whites in American life. He lived to see his own achievements tainted with racial humiliation and sometimes misused not to advance other blacks, as he had dreamed, but to put them down.

Childhood

The plantation where his grandmother left young Frederick Bailey that afternoon in 1824 was one of Maryland's most prosperous—10,000 acres of flat, fertile land. . . .

He became the companion and, surreptitiously, a careful student of the Lloyd family's youngest boy. The great house, not the slave quarters, was to be his chosen element.

His mind also opened quickly to the horrific gulf between these worlds. Apart from cold and hunger, Douglass suffered little personal mistreatment on the Lloyd plantation. But in *Narrative of the Life of Frederick Douglass*, published in 1845, he recounted the violence all around him.

One incident burned itself into the child's memory. Frederick was the property not of the Lloyds themselves but of their head manager, Captain Aaron Anthony, the man his grandmother had spoken of as "old master." His modest brick house . . . still stands, on the plantation farm road, but the site of the kitchen building where Frederick slept is now just a faint depression in the grass. . . .

For much of his childhood, [Douglass's mother] was a field hand on a distant farm, and the memory of her infrequent visits remained achingly fresh. She died before he was 10, without confirming or denying the rumor in the slave quarters that Captain Anthony was his father. Slavery, he wrote, "left me without an intelligible beginning in the world."

Douglass' mother became an almost mythic figure for him. He attributed the love of letters for which he became famous largely to this "unprotected and uncultivated" field hand, who had somehow learned to read. He also credited his grandmother's valuable example. Though illiterate, she had won a measure of indepen-

dence by her practical skills at farming and at manufac-
turing the long drift nets used for harvesting shad and
herring from the Tuckahoe. Recognizing something
special in Frederick, perhaps including kinship, Captain Anthony's family soon spirited him away from the
brutality of the plantation to be a house servant for
their in-laws in Baltimore.

There, Sophia Auld started to teach the 8-year-old
his letters, but her husband quickly stopped her.
"Learning would spoil the best nigger in the world," he
said, as if Frederick could not hear every word. Education "would forever unfit him to be a slave. . . . If you
learn him how to read, he'll want to know how to write;
and this accomplished, he'll be running away with himself." Douglass later described it as "the first decidedly
antislavery lecture" he ever heard.

The boy set out, against all odds, to educate himself.
Put to work in a local shipyard, he noticed that the car-
penters chalked each sawed-out timber with initials,
like "sf" for "starboard for-ward," indicating its eventual placement in the ship. Copying these letters on a
fence board, he challenged his white playmates to beat
his penmanship and thus inveigled them into helping
him learn the alphabet.

He also listened as they memorized speeches for
school from a standard anthology of the day, *The
Columbian Orator.* Words like "emancipation" . . . and
"equality" . . . fired his imagination. When he had accumulated 30 cents from polishing boots, he bought a
secondhand copy for himself. There he found the
three-page "Dialogue Between A Master and Slave," in
which the slave argues that kind treatment can never
compensate for depriving a man of liberty. When the
master declares that "Providence" has made him a
slave, the slave replies that Providence "has also given
me legs to escape with."

Frederick would carry with him the message, the rhetorical method and his copy of *The Columbian Orator* when he made his own escape eight years later. Using the borrowed papers of a free black seaman, he took a train north.

Speaking from Experience

By 1841, the fugitive Frederick Bailey had become "Frederick Douglass" (a name borrowed from a poem by Sir Walter Scott). He had married Anna Murray, a free black woman from Baltimore who had helped him escape, and they were living in Massachusetts. He shoveled coal and dug cellars for a living, and stoked his wrath against slavery by reading William Lloyd Garrison's abolitionist newspaper, *The Liberator.* He also preached abolition to other blacks in his local church.

Garrison, the leader of the antislavery movement, heard Douglass speak in Nantucket in 1841; the group that Garrison led immediately hired him as a lecturer. For the struggling antislavery movement of the 1840s, Douglass was, in his own words, a "brand new fact," the first fugitive-slave lecturer: "Up to that time, a colored man was deemed a fool who confessed himself a runaway slave, not only because of the danger to which he exposed himself of being retaken, but because it was a confession of very low origin!"

Frederick Douglass was unafraid to say just how low slavery had set him, and he made a virtue of overcoming it. He had spent the years before his escape working both in Baltimore and in the fields of the Eastern Shore. He could recount the horrors of slavery in the most moving language many listeners had ever heard, in a voice that could be conversational one moment, and the next, "roll out full and deep" as organ music. "I have come to tell you something about slavery—what I know of it, as I have felt it," he began. Other abolition-

ists could not speak "from experience; they cannot refer you to a back covered with scars, as I can; . . . my
blood has sprung out as the lash embedded itself in my
flesh." And he added, from a deeper vein of emotion,
"the whip we can bear without a murmur, compared to
the idea of separation . . . the agony of the mother when
parting from her children.". . .

The account of his life in slavery was so detailed and
accurate that Frederick Douglass faced renewed danger
of being kidnapped back to the South. On the advice of
his mentors in the antislavery movement, he sailed for
Europe—and was nearly heaved overboard en route by
proslavery passengers who did not want him to lecture.
The incident made headlines on his arrival, and his lectures over the next 21 months enabled him to return to
the United States as an international celebrity—and,
literally, as his own man. British supporters raised $700
to buy his freedom from the Auld family. They also allowed him for the first time in his life to eat a meal, register at a hotel, go to church or visit a friend free from
the dismal American refrain, "We don't allow niggers
in here!"

Back in this country, Douglass moved his wife and
their children away from Massachusetts, where white
abolitionist leaders still regarded him more as a hired
performer than as their peer. He established his own
newspaper, the *North Star*, in Rochester, New York. He
and Anna made their new home a refuge for the steady
traffic of runaway slaves who were following the underground railroad to Canada. A white Englishwoman
named Julia Griffiths managed the publishing business
during his frequent absences on the lecture circuit. She
also became his intellectual companion, and their appearance together on the streets of New York City
drew obscene shouts and a physical assault. The friendship developed as Douglass and his wife were drifting

apart emotionally. As he moved out into the world of politics and letters, Anna Douglass withdrew into child-rearing and her garden. Books were his private passion, but she could read only two words: "Fred" and "Douglass."

The Conscience of the War

The voice of Frederick Douglass grew more powerful through the violent decade leading up to the Civil War. Most abolitionists abhorred the U.S. Constitution, which treated the slave as three-fifths of a human being. But Douglass now declared that the constitutional oath to "secure the Blessings of Liberty to ourselves and our Posterity" was, in fact, an oath to free the slaves. He advocated emancipation within the political system, and despite his sympathies, he refrained from openly advocating a slave rebellion. Better than most abolitionists, he could imagine the bloody consequences for blacks.

Seeing the wild impracticality of the scheme, he refused to join his friend John Brown in a suicidal raid on the federal arsenal at Harpers Ferry in 1859. The raid, of course, failed. One of the martyrs of the event, Shields Green, had traveled with Douglass to meet with Brown before the raid, and when Douglass resolved to leave, Green stayed behind. "I b'lieve I'll go wid de ole man," he said mildly. His death and the others at Harpers Ferry aroused the nation. Douglass later remarked, "I could live for the slave; John Brown could die for him." He was soon battering his way to the podium through a crowd of racist hecklers to advocate death to slaveholders, death to slave-catchers, and war.

"I believe in agitation," he declared, and the Civil War did not change that. When President [Abraham] Lincoln found it expedient to wage war to preserve the Union, not to end slavery, Douglass denounced the Ad-

ministration for "moral blindness . . . and helpless im-
becility." He helped maintain the political pressure
which, together with military expediency (and moral vision), induced Lincoln to issue the Emancipation
Proclamation on January 1, 1863. Douglass called it "a
day for poetry and song," wept with fellow abolitionists—and continued to agitate. He set to work recruit-
ing more than a hundred men, including two of his own
sons, to make the emancipation of slaves a reality under
the banner of the U.S. Army's newly formed 54th
Massachusetts, the first black regiment. Then Douglass
went to the White House to agitate on behalf of black
soldiers.

Lincoln greeted Douglass warmly and listened to his
complaints: black soldiers got half the pay of white soldiers, could not become officers and faced the added
peril of being put to death if captured by the Confed-
erates. Some of the soldiers Douglass had recruited had
already fought and died at Fort Wagner; prisoners from
the 54th had been sold into slavery. Douglass came
away impressed with Lincoln's sincerity and convinced
he would act—always within the limits of practical politics—to protect the black soldier.

Back on the lecture circuit, Douglass remained the
conscience of the war effort, keeping his listeners focused on the high moral ground of freedom versus slavery. "No war but an Abolition war," he declared in
1864, when Lincoln and the Union wavered, "no peace
but an Abolition peace; liberty for all, chains for none;
the black man a soldier in war; a laborer in peace; a
voter at the South as well as at the North. . . . Such, fel-
low-citizens, is my idea for the mission of this war."

The decades after the war brought Douglass honors
but seemed to take away his spirit. He worked tirelessly
for the passage in 1870 of the 15th Amendment to the
Constitution. Black men now had the vote, but that did

not prevent them from being "mobbed, beaten, shot, stabbed, hanged, burnt . . . the target of all that is malignant in the North and all that is murderous in the South." His own home in Rochester was destroyed by arson in 1872. The postwar years saw the use of every imaginable device, legal or otherwise, to keep blacks from exercising their new rights.

Douglass moved his family to Washington, D.C. in search of a public office worthy of his abilities. As a 19-year-old slave he'd had the audacity to dream out loud among his free black friends that he would some day become a U.S. Senator. Now he became president of the Freedman's Bank, just in time to take the blame when it defaulted on the meager savings of its black account holders. He went on to become Marshal of the District of Columbia, a job that gave Douglass status and the power to employ blacks. But this appointment of the most prominent black man in America also served as a screen for the decision of the [President Rutherford B.] Hayes Administration to withdraw vital military protection of blacks from some areas of the South.

In 1877 Frederick and Anna Douglass bought a beautiful house on a hilltop in the rural southeastern corner of the city. He had the satisfaction of knowing that a previous owner had tried to prevent the property from ever being owned by blacks or Irish; from his porch, he could look down across the Anacostia River onto the great dome of the Capitol. That same autumn, he went back to the Eastern Shore and located the site of his grandmother's slave cabin, near a familiar-looking cedar tree. Douglass scooped up some of the soil to scatter at his new home, which he called Cedar Hill.

Having triumphed in the great fight over slavery, Douglass could afford to be magnanimous with his white connections on the Eastern Shore—too magnanimous for his critics. He sipped Madeira on the porch of the great house of the Lloyd plantation and spoke of "gratitude" at his reunion with the Lloyd family. He had an emotional meeting with Thomas Auld, one of his former owners, now on his deathbed; he expressed regret that he had publicly accused Auld of "cruel" treatment of his grandmother, whom he had mistakenly thought was one of Auld's slaves. Auld wept and told him in turn that "had I been in your place, I should have done as you did."

Anna Douglass died in 1882, and two years later Douglass married Helen Pitts, a clerk in his office. She was a white woman, and his own family took the marriage as a repudiation of blacks. Her father, who had been an abolitionist, also rejected the marriage, refusing to allow Douglass into his house. Of their outside critics, Douglass inquired with simple dignity, "What business has the world with the color of my wife?" Helen remarked, "I was not afraid to marry the man I loved because of his color." It was a happy marriage, and the criticism did not prevent Douglass from being named Minister to Haiti in 1889.

Opening Doors

Near the end of his life, Douglass also formed a vital friendship with another woman. Ida B. Wells, a young black writer in Memphis, had published a detailed account of the extent to which the lynching of blacks had become a form of social control in the South. "What a revelation of existing conditions," Douglass remarked, when he read her work. Like the younger Douglass, Wells fearlessly named names, places and motives. When they met, they would also share intellectual interests and a combative zeal. Wells later recalled going to lunch with him one day after a speech. She mentioned that a nearby restaurant did not serve blacks. "Mr. Douglass, in his vigorous way, grasped my arm and said, 'Come, let's go there' . . . and we sauntered into the Boston Oyster House as if it were an everyday occurrence, cocked and primed for a fight if necessary." Fortunately for the restaurant, Douglass received a hero's welcome.

Another time, when Wells was a guest in the Douglass home, she received an invitation to undertake a lecture tour in Britain. Douglass encouraged her to go, saying, "You go my child; you are the one to go, for you have the story to tell." It was, Wells wrote, "like an open door in a stone wall" of public indifference. She passed through it and carried her mentor's struggle for racial equality well into the 20th century.

Douglass himself found a new opening in his protegee's example. In January 1894, full of his old majesty and wrath, he delivered one of his greatest speeches at a church in Washington, D.C. In "The Lessons of the Hour," Douglass carefully dissected the ways prejudice worked to keep blacks down. "A white man has but to blacken his face and commit a crime," he said, "to have some Negro lynched in his stead. An abandoned woman has only to start to cry that she has been insulted by a black man, to have him arrested and summarily murdered by the mob." More than 850 Southern blacks had been executed by officials or lynched by mobs from 1890 to 1892 alone. The usual trumped-up charge of sexual assault on white women, he said, was shrewdly calculated to drive from the suspect "all sympathy and all fair play." Moreover, it was a charge not merely against the individual but against all blacks: "When a white man steals, robs or murders, his crime is visited upon his own head alone. . . . When [a black man] commits a crime the whole race is made to suffer."

The so-called race problem, Douglass said, "cannot be solved by keeping the Negro poor, degraded, ignorant and half-starved. . . . It cannot be solved by keeping the wages of the laborer back by fraud. . . . It cannot be done by ballot-box stuffing . . . or by confusing Negro voters by cunning devices. It can, however, be done, and very easily done. . . . Let the white people of the North and South conquer their prejudices. . . .

"Time and strength are not equal to the task before me," he concluded. "But could I be heard by this great nation, I would call to mind the sublime and glorious truths with which, at its birth, it sainted a listening world. . . . Put away your race prejudice. Banish the idea that one class must rule over another. Recognize . . . that the rights of the humblest citizen are as worthy of protection as are those of the highest, and . . . your Republic will stand and flourish forever."

A little more than a year later, as he recounted for his wife the events of the women's rights rally he had attended that afternoon, Douglass sank to the floor of their home and died. His body was taken to Rochester for burial.

The gravestone is curiously generic for a man whose life was full of well-chosen words, and historians now know that the year of his birth, which eluded him till the end, is wrong. The stone reads: "To the memory of Frederick Douglass—1817–1895." A visitor paying homage might think, instead, of the newspaper called the *North Star* that a visionary, headstrong young man once published in the city. The title came from a fugitive-slave song. Frederick Douglass could sing the words with a truth matched by few Americans before him or after: "I kept my eye on the bright north star, and thought of liberty."

Susan B. Anthony: A Pioneer in Woman's Rights

Sara Ann McGill

Sara Ann McGill details the activism of Susan B. Anthony, who started petitions, made speeches, lobbied Congress, and created her own publication to fight social injustice. McGill claims that Anthony's passion for human rights began at antislavery meetings, but her focus later shifted from abolition to woman's rights and their "unfair social standing." Feeling that concerned women needed a voice in government, Anthony joined friend Elizabeth Cady Stanton to lead the women's movement, focusing on a woman's right to vote. Anthony died before the Nineteenth Amendment, giving women the legal right to vote, was passed in 1920. McGill wrote this article for the journal *Women's History*. McGill has written several books and articles on historic figures.

❧ ❧ ❧

Susan Brownell Anthony, an important suffragette and abolitionist, was born on February 15, 1820 to a Quaker family in the small town of Adams, Massachu-

Sara Ann McGill, "Susan B. Anthony," *Women's History*, 2002, p. 59. Copyright © 2002 by Indiana University Press. Reproduced by permission.

setts. When she was seventeen, her family moved to Battenville, New York where they did their best to survive during the economic depression. Her father soon had to declare bankruptcy and they lost their house. In 1845, they moved to Rochester, New York and Anthony took a job as a schoolteacher at Canajoharie Academy in order to help her family, who was deeply in debt.

Anthony's passion for human rights issues began in her Quaker home in Rochester, which became a gathering place for anti-slavery meetings. She was also taught by her faith that drinking alcohol was wrong. Believing that alcohol was "sinful," she also supported the temperance movement. Her focus later shifted from abolition and prohibition to women's rights, but she never completely abandoned any cause and divided her time according to what she felt was most important. Anthony toured the nation in support of various social causes—starting petitions, making speeches, and lobbying Congress. She even created her own publication in 1868 called *The Revolution*, which she used to discuss injustice.

Anthony's Activism

Anthony's passion for the temperance movement launched her public career. While teaching at Canajoharie Academy, she joined the Daughters of Temperance, whose purpose was to make the public aware of the results of excessive consumption of alcohol on individuals and families. The first public speech Anthony made was at a meeting of the Daughters in 1848. The next year her leadership qualities were recognized when she was voted president of her local branch of the Daughters of Temperance. Though she shone as an inexhaustible leader in her own group, she encountered many obstacles. At a Sons of Temperance meeting held in 1853 in Albany she was refused the right to speak.

The Sons instructed her to "listen and learn" instead. That same year she and a friend, Elizabeth Cady Stanton, submitted a petition signed by 28,000 people, asking that the sales of alcohol in New York be limited. Anthony was infuriated by the State Legislature's response. In their eyes the petition was meaningless because most of those who signed it were women and children.

Anthony's anger against slavery was most likely a result of the abolitionist meetings held in her family's home in Rochester. A few dignitaries, such as Frederick Douglass and William Lloyd Garrison, were known to attend these particular meetings on occasion. By 1856 Anthony had become a paid agent for the Anti-Slavery Society, working primarily as an organizer and publicist. She was publicly mocked and threatened because of her work, but she was not deterred. In 1861 she organized a speaking campaign against slavery that started in Buffalo and finished in Albany. When the Thirteenth Amendment, which abolished slavery, was presented to legislators in 1863, Anthony supported it wholeheartedly.

The Women's Movement

In observing the inhumane treatment of slaves, many female abolitionists began to notice their own unequal status as women in the eyes of the government and society. Anthony, among others, had good reason to protest against the unfair social standing of women. The obstacles she encountered in her temperance work convinced her that women needed to have a voice in government. Her friendship with Elizabeth Cady Stanton, a fellow abolitionist and an experienced supporter of women's rights, influenced Anthony as well. In 1852 the Women's Rights Convention met for the first time.

Stanton and Anthony became co-leaders in the women's movement, though each seemed to have a different agenda. For example, Stanton, as a married woman, found the cultural mores surrounding marriage particularly exasperating. She resented the fact that a woman was expected to give up her own last name to take on her husband's. More mundane issues, such as standards for women's dress, bothered Anthony. The long and bulky skirts women wore during her time were impossible to keep clean and they kept women from working with machinery. Such clothing prevented women from doing men's jobs and thus could not make men's salaries [in the workforce]. In protest, Anthony abandoned the traditional garb of a woman for a time and donned a bloomer uniform.

Generally, Anthony worked alongside Stanton. Together they co-authored an "Appeal to the Women of the Republic" in 1863. Much later, in 1887, all groups working for the enfranchisement of women combined into the National American Women's Suffrage Association (NAWSA), with Stanton as the president and Anthony as vice-president.

After the Civil War ended in 1865 and the controversies of Reconstruction occupied the nation, the women's movement lost some momentum. People were not as willing to question fundamental traditions. Anthony felt she was forced to choose one issue that was the most important; she chose to fight for women's right to vote. In 1869, Anthony and Stanton devised a strategy to help in this endeavor; they would fight to change the laws one state at a time. That year Wyoming became the first state to allow women to vote.

In 1872, Anthony and her three sisters decided to cast a ballot. Her boldness was encouraged by Victoria Woodhull's recent argument before Congress that a woman's right to vote was inherent in the Constitution. But Anthony was not successful in convincing local authorities of that fact, and she was arrested. An Albany court indicted her and she was brought before another court in Canandaigua the next year. The judge presiding over her case actually told the jury not to bother with deliberation and to find her guilty. She was fined $100, which she refused to pay. The judge could have sent her to prison for such an action, but did not, thus preventing her from appealing her case before another judge.

The Later Years

Despite the many frustrations Anthony encountered, she continued to make speeches and write petitions. In 1887 she and Stanton did succeed in leading the NAWSA, with Anthony taking over as its president when Stanton retired in 1892. She stepped down from this position in 1900, only to officiate the International Council of Women in Berlin of 1904. The following year, she met with President Theodore Roosevelt to discuss the possibility of an amendment that would nationally legalize women's vote. In 1906, Anthony turned 86 and at her birthday party she made her most famous speech, entitled "Failure is Impossible." That same year, she died at her home in Rochester, N.Y. She did not live to see the passage of the [Nineteenth] Amendment, which gave all women in the United States the legal right to vote, in 1920, fourteen years after her death.

Martin Luther King Jr.: Civil Rights Activist

Russel Moldovan

Sacrificing his life to secure a more just and inclusive society, Martin Luther King Jr. stands out as one of the most important leaders in human rights. King became involved in the fight when pastors in Montgomery, Alabama, organized a bus boycott to fight discrimination. These pastors unanimously elected King to head the boycott, and he immediately saw his human rights activities as an extension of his ministry. According to King, Jesus Christ provided the motivation for the fight, and Mohandas Gandhi provided the method. King followed Gandhi's example of nonviolence, leading sit-ins and rallies to help break down walls of oppression for black citizens around the world. When attention for the movement he championed increased national hostilities, King was assassinated in 1968.

Russel Moldovan highlights King's life and cause in the following article. Moldovan is pastor of Blanchard Church of Christ in Pennsylvania and author of *Martin Luther King Jr.: An Oral History of His Religious Witness and His Life*.

❧   ❧   ❧

No Christian played a more prominent role in the century's most significant social justice movement than Martin Luther King, Jr.

"We must keep God in the forefront. Let us be Christian in all our actions." So spoke the newly elected president of the Montgomery Improvement Association, which had just been organized to lead a bus boycott to protest segregated seating in the city buses. The president, and new pastor of Dexter Avenue Baptist, went on to say that blacks must not hate their white opponents. "Love is one of the pinnacle parts of the Christian faith. There is another side called justice, and justice is really love in calculation."

And so began his public role in the civil rights movement of the 1950s and 1960s. The movement produced scores of men and women who risked their lives to secure a more just and inclusive society, but the name Martin Luther King, Jr., stands out among them all. As historian Mark Noll put it, "He was beyond question the most important Christian voice in the most important social protest movement after World War II."

He was born in Atlanta, Georgia, in 1929 as Michael King, but in 1935 his father changed both of their names to Martin Luther to honor the German Protestant Reformer. The precocious Martin skipped two grades, and by age 15, had passed the entrance exam to the predominantly black Morehouse College. There King felt drawn into pastoral ministry: "My call to the ministry was not a miraculous or supernatural something," he said. "On the contrary it was an inner urge calling me to serve humanity."

From Morehouse he moved on to Crozer Theological Seminary (Chester, Pennsylvania) and Boston University, both predominantly white and liberal, where he studied Euro-American philosophers and theologians.

King was especially taken with social gospel champion Walter Rauschenbusch, whom King said "had done a great service for the Christian church by insisting that the gospel deals with the whole man, not only his soul but his body."

King also admired the nonviolent civil disobedience of Mahatma Gandhi: "Gandhi was probably the first person in history to lift the love ethic of Jesus above mere interaction between individuals to a powerful and effective social force on a large scale." King also believed "Christ furnished the spirit and motivation, and Gandhi furnished the method."

King left Boston in 1953 with his new wife Coretta to pastor at Dexter Baptist Church in Montgomery, Alabama. When he took the position, he said, he had not "the slightest idea that I would later become involved in a crisis in which nonviolent resistance would be applicable."

In December 1955, a young Montgomery woman named Rosa Parks was arrested for refusing to relinquish her bus seat to a white man. Local pastors rallied the black community for a city-wide bus boycott, named themselves the Montgomery Improvement Association, and unanimously elected King as president.

King immediately implemented his ideas, insisting throughout the boycott on a policy of nonviolence despite the threat of white violence. Even after his home was bombed, King forbade those guarding his home from carrying guns; instead, he told his followers, "Keep moving . . . with the faith that what we are doing is right, and with the even greater faith that God is with us in the struggle."

Throughout the Montgomery campaign, critics complained about the ordained clergy's involvement in "earthly, temporal matters." King, however, believed "this view of religion . . . was too confined." He saw his civil rights activity as an extension of his ministry: "The Christian gospel is a two-way road. On the one hand, it seeks to change the souls of men, and thereby unite them with God; on the other hand, it seeks to change the environmental conditions of men so the soul will have a chance after it is changed."

When a year later the boycott succeeded in ending bus discrimination, King was propelled into the national limelight. In 1957 he helped found the Southern Christian Leadership Conference (SCLC), an umbrella for civil rights organizations. The next year, he published his first of seven books, *Stride Toward Freedom*.

Along with increasing national attention came increasing hostility: while autographing his book in a department store, an assailant stabbed King in the chest with a letter opener. It took some time to get him proper care, and his surgeon later told him, "If you had sneezed during all those hours of waiting, your aorta would have been punctured and you would have drowned in your own blood."

Leaders of the civil rights movement Martin Luther King Jr. and Malcolm X wait for a press conference in 1964. They shared similar views on civil and human rights.

In 1959 King moved to Atlanta to become co-pastor with his father at Ebenezer Baptist Church. The next years saw him organizing peaceful demonstrations in Atlanta (1960), Albany (Georgia, 1961), Birmingham (1963), St. Augustine (Florida, 1964), and Selma (1965). King received death threats, was once stoned, was arrested several times and held in solitary confinement.

In addition, after King criticized the FBI in 1964 for cooperating with segregation authorities, the FBI stepped up its surveillance of King. A mixture of politics and personal animosity prompted FBI chief J. Edgar Hoover to try to discredit King as a womanizer and communist. There was, unfortunately, substance to the first charge but not the second (the most that can be said is that King's early advisers had formerly been members of the Communist Party). Hoover called King "the most notorious liar in the country," and the FBI went so far as to send a letter to King suggesting he commit suicide.

King became increasingly troubled with the dichotomy between his private and public selves, and the burden of leading the SCLC often seemed overwhelming. But his preaching continued to inspire his followers. His greatest oratorical moment came on August 28, 1963, when 250,000 demonstrators gathered at the Lincoln Memorial in Washington, D.C. All speakers had their speeches pre-approved, but in King's original, the now-famous phrase, "I have a dream," never appeared. King was the last speaker of the long, hot day. He noted the fatigued state of his audience, and he remembered a phrase he'd heard spoken by a young woman who had some months earlier led a service at the remains of a torched church.

"I have a dream," he began, "that one day on the red hills of Georgia, sons of former slaves and sons of former slave-owners will be able to sit down together at the table of brotherhood. . . .

"I have a dream my four little children will one day live in a nation where they will not be judged by the color of their skin but by the content of their character."

In 1964, at the height of his influence, King became *Time* magazine's first black "Man of the Year," then the youngest person ever to win the Nobel Peace Prize. He donated the prize money ($54,600) to civil rights organizations.

Beginning in 1965, King's popularity waned as his "dream" grew to include peace in Vietnam. With this, most of white America, as well as many African Americans, distanced themselves from King. But he refused to soften his language about the war: "On some positions, cowardice asks the question, is it expedient? And then expedience comes along and asks the question—is it politic? Vanity asks the question—is it popular? Conscience asks the question—is it right?"

In spring of 1968, King was in Memphis to help with a sanitation strike. On April 3, he told his audience, "I may not get there with you, but I want you to know that tonight that we as a people will get to the promised land." The following day, James Earl Ray shot and killed King as he stood on the balcony of the Lorraine Motel.

The nation mourned King's death, and the civil rights movement fragmented irreversibly. King's influence may have waned in the last two years of his life, but 20 years after his death, his legacy was deemed so crucial to the nation's history that a national holiday was named after him.

Iqbal Masih: Martyr for Child Labor

Timothy Ryan

Murdered at the age of twelve in April 1995 for his activism, Iqbal Masih had become an international symbol against child labor and inhumane working conditions. Masih spent six years chained to a carpet loom bonded as a slave for his parent's debt of sixteen dollars. After seeing a poster from the Bonded Labor Liberation Foundation (BLLF) declaring child labor illegal, Masih secretly contacted the organization and was rescued. Spending the next two years testifying before the International Labor Organization as president of the BLLF children's section, Masih became a crusader against the inhumane conditions associated with the third-world traditions of bonded child labor.

Timothy Ryan, an American Federation of Labor-Congress of Industrial Organizations (AFL-CIO) representative in South Asia, highlights Masih's call to human rights vigilance.

❧ ❧ ❧

Anyone who knew Iqbal Masih, the 12-year-old boy . . . assassinated in Lahore, Pakistan, by someone be-

Timothy Ryan, "Iqbal Masih's Life—A Call to Human Rights Vigilance," *Christian Science Monitor*, vol. 87, May 3, 1995, p. 18. Copyright © 1995 by The Christian Science Publishing Society. All rights reserved. Reproduced by permission.

lieved to be a feudal landlord and carpet manufacturer, was struck by his brilliance.

I don't simply mean his intellectual abilities, though once rescued from slavery at a carpet loom this young activist demonstrated a tremendous aptitude for learning. He went through five years of school curriculum in three. Although malnutrition and abuse left him, at the age of 12, physically smaller and more frail than my nine-year-old daughter, it was clear that his mind, his ambition, and his spirit burned brightly.

When I saw him last December [1994] in Karachi on his return from the United States, where he received a Reebok Human Rights Award, he was filled with the excitement of his first airplane ride, a new Instamatic camera, his visit with other schoolchildren in Boston, and the unimaginable promise that one day he might attend a university. Brandeis University had pledged to give a four-year scholarship to Iqbal when he finished his studies in Pakistan.

Then someone motivated by greed, by fear, by hatred, pulled the trigger of a shotgun and obliterated this promise.

I first met Iqbal [in 1994] through my work with the Bonded Labor Liberation Front [BLLF], as a representative of the AFL-CIO in South Asia.

The BLLF has worked dauntlessly for years to free thousands of bonded and child laborers, Iqbal among them. After working six years at a carpet loom, starting at the age of four, Iqbal was rescued by the BLLF when he was 10.

Iqbal's rescue was due in no small part to his own guts. Last December he told me that one day two years ago in the village where he was enslaved as a carpet weaver, he saw BLLF posters declaring that bonded and child labor was illegal under Pakistan law and secretly contacted BLLF activists. At the risk of his own life, Iqbal led the BLLF to the carpet looms where they rescued hundreds of children, who might still be in slavery if not for his courage.

It seems medieval, and perhaps it is, but for years carpet manufacturers, brick kiln owners, landowners, and manufacturers of sporting goods and other products in Pakistan have maintained an unrelenting grip on bonded laborers and children. Some estimates run as high as 20 million bonded and child laborers. At least half a million children are employed in the carpet trade alone.

Because of the current tension between Islamic and Christian communities in Pakistan, some apologists want to paint the killing of Iqbal as a purely religious matter. On one level this is a mere smoke screen. But on a more complex and sinister level, there is some connection between the fact that Iqbal was Christian and the fact that he was pressed into slavery in the first place.

Iqbal's story has an economic and political subtext. Politicians and businessmen in Pakistan form a tight web of relationships based on kin, clan, and caste. They count on family members who occupy positions of authority in local, provincial, national, and police bodies to look the other way when laws are violated, or, in many cases, to actively participate in crimes against workers and minorities.

Poverty is often the surface excuse for a problem that has deeper roots. It's a fallacy to see Iqbal's death solely as the result of brutal economics, rather than the outcome of broader, more pervasive violations of fundamental human rights.

On one level Iqbal's story is surely economic—poor people have less education, less income, less power than the rich. Even though it was outlawed in 1992 under Pakistan's Bonded Labor Abolition Act, the "advance" system that bonds people to their employers continues unabated. This system ensnared Iqbal at the age of four.

Iqbal Masih

Pharis J. Harvey, executive director of the International Labor Rights Education and Research Fund and a cochair of the Child Labor Coalition, comments on Iqbal Masih's life and death as a crusader against child labor.

After being chained to a carpet loom for half his life, Iqbal Masih is dead at the age of 12. He was killed in the dark of night on Easter Sunday as he and two cousins were taking supper to a relative working in a field outside of Lahore, Pakistan. A perfunctory one-paragraph police report said the boys had surprised a local farmworker named Muhammed Ashraf, alias "Hero," in a compromising act with a donkey, "whereupon Ashraf took out a 12-bore gun and fired straight at Iqbal Masih."

Iqbal died immediately of massive hemorrhaging from 120 pellet wounds to his back, buttocks and legs. Ashraf disappeared. Iqbal's cousins and mother, members of Pakistan's impoverished Christian minority, fled for their lives to the protection of the Bonded Labor Liberation Front of Pakistan (BLLF-P), the organization that had liberated [Iqbal in 1992]. This amazingly courageous child was known around the world. After his rescue from the carpet loom, he became a dauntless crusader against bonded servitude in Pakistan's carpet in-

The BLLF has taken some cases to court, but police and employer intimidation, along with judges' unwillingness to enforce the law, has prevented any prosecutions under the 1992 law.

It's at a deeper, generally hidden level that Iqbal's tragedy intersects with millions of Pakistani citizens and helps to explain the oppressive social and cultural patterns that are partly responsible for his death.

The fact is, most people who are bonded and en-

dustry, in which half a million or more children toil under inhumane conditions. . . . He traveled to Europe to testify before the International Labor Organization, and was president of BLLF's children's section. . . .

As Christians, the Masih family is among the poorest, most oppressed in officially Muslim Pakistan. One can only imagine the family's anguish when they were forced by circumstance to place their four-year-old son in a carpet factory, bonded by a loan of a paltry $16. For six years Iqbal was shackled to the carpet loom by day and paid one rupee ($0.03) per day. When he was liberated by the BLLF-P in 1992, he had supposedly accumulated a debt to his master of 13,000 Rp. ($419).

Millions of other Pakistan children toil under similar conditions. A campaign to label carpets produced without child labor could press the Pakistani government to end the abuse. The Rugmark campaign, building on the awareness generated by Iqbal's death, could lead to basic education, agrarian reform, enforcement of laws banning child and bonded labor, rehabilitation for victims and development assistance from U.S. and international agencies. If the campaign is to succeed, and if Iqbal's death is to gain any meaning for the children he tried to save, adults must take up his cause in the corridors of power and in the showrooms of the carpet trade.

Pharis J. Harvey, "Iqbal's Death," *Christian Century*, May 24, 1995, p. 557.

slaved are converted Muslims, indigenous tribal people, Hindus, and Christans—in short, anyone outside the mainstream of Sunni Islamic society. This insight reveals the intrinsic link between "economic" or "labor" issues and pervasive problems of intolerance and discrimination based on race, language, and ethnicity.

So we're not just talking here about poverty and economic hardship, or one brave little boy's death. We're talking about enslavement based on race and language and religion, about the treatment of human beings as commodities, as slave labor, and the slow grinding to death of people who not only are denied economic advancement, but also a chance at education, decent housing, clean water—the things that make life livable.

Iqbal's death must have a greater meaning beyond the tragedy of a bright meteor snuffed out by greed and corruption. His experience implores us to look beyond "poverty" or "economic hardship" as an explanation of why so many men, women, and children in traditional societies are exploited—to see the rights of child workers and bonded workers as part of a continuum of overall human rights that must be defended at all costs.

CHAPTER

4

Profiles · in · History

Champions for
the Oppressed

Eleanor Roosevelt: The Human Touch

Labor Today

Although Eleanor Roosevelt grew up in a world of wealth and privilege, she committed her life to improving human rights. In the following viewpoint, *Labor Today* describes Roosevelt as the "First Lady of the World." Years before she became first lady of the United States, Roosevelt used her influence to promote black civil rights, equal opportunity in employment, and equal pay for equal work. She helped to reform working conditions in the New York garment district and was instrumental in providing legislative and financial support to working women. She was a leader in adopting the Universal Declaration of Human Rights issued from the United Nations to better human rights conditions around the world. According to this article, Roosevelt left an imprint in the area of human rights politics that affected all societies around the world. *Labor Today* is a biannual journal that deals with employment issues.

❦   ❦   ❦

To the Depression generation, she was a saint: to their children she is forgotten. Eleanor Roosevelt wife of four-

Labor Today, "Eleanor Roosevelt—A First Lady, Unionist, Fighter for Peace," vol. 29, Spring/Summer 1990, p. 14. Copyright © 1990 by *Labor Today*. Reproduced by permission.

term President Franklin D. Roosevelt, etched a career in government and foreign service that few people have ever matched. Her support of the American worker and of trade unions is an important part of her legacy.

Born on October 11, 1884 to the nephew of President Theodore Roosevelt, Eleanor grew up in the world of Victorian wealth and privilege. Yet she never fully accepted the life of the rich debutante. Instead, she took part in the world of settlement house work and social reform.

She joined the National Consumer's League at the age of 18. High on the agenda of the League was improving the health and safety of clothing workshops and sweatshops, where women worked. Eleanor visited these unsafe workplaces and witnessed the misery of garment workers firsthand. She taught at the Rivington Street Settlement House, a building located in one of the worst slums in New York's Lower East Side and became a well-known reformer.

Standing Together

In 1905, she married her cousin Franklin Roosevelt, whose political career was just beginning. In 1922, she joined the Women's Trade Union League, where, along with a number of other well-connected women, she provided legislative and financial support to working-class women. It is said that her interest in labor and unions grew out of her involvement with his group.

When her husband became stricken with polio in 1922, Eleanor became Franklin's most important political representative. Catapulted into the political arena, she quickly learned how to use politics to further her own political agenda. She was the head of a delegation to the Democratic convention in 1924 and fought unsuccessfully for equal pay legislation, a child labor amendment, and other reform measures.

Identifying with the Masses

Biographer Blanche Wiesen Cook comments on Eleanor Roosevelt's lifelong commitment to human rights, saying no group was beyond her concern.

[Eleanor Roosevelt (ER)] was eight when her mother, Anna, died at the age of twenty-nine; and ten when her beloved father, Elliott, died of alcoholism at the age of thirty-four. From then on, she identified particularly with people in want, in need, in trouble, and devoted her time especially to those on the margins, or beyond its borders. After each visit to women's prisons, ER left haunted by the feeling that she could have been any one of the women on the inside.

There was no group beyond her concern, no people outside her imagination, no category of outsiders designated for abandonment. Every life was sacred and worthy, to be improved by education, employment, health care, affordable housing. Her goal was simple, a life of dignity and decency for all. She was uninterested in complex theories, and demanded action for betterment. She feared violent revolution, but was not afraid of socialism—and she courted radicals. . . .

She understood, above all, that politics is not an isolated individualist adventure. She sought alliances, created community, worked with movements for justice and peace. Against great odds, and under terrific pressure, she refused to withdraw from controversy. She brought her network of agitators and activists into the White House, and never considered a political setback a permanent defeat. She enjoyed the game, and weathered the abuse. Energized by her friends and allies, she devoted some part of every day to the business of others.

Blanche Wiesen Cook, *Eleanor Roosevelt: The Defining Years, vol. 2, 1933–1938.* New York: Viking, 1999, pp. 4, 7.

After Franklin's election as New York's governor in 1928, Eleanor persuaded her husband to appoint Frances Perkins, a woman, as commissioner of industrial relations. Perkins would later become Labor Secretary in the first Roosevelt administration in the White House.

Eleanor walked many picket lines. In 1931, she addressed a group of striking Fifth Avenue dressmakers, urging them to continue their struggle and efforts to organize.

Ten years later, as First Lady, she told striking members of the International Brotherhood of Electrical Workers at the Leviton factory in Brooklyn that it was important to stand together "to gain those things, materially and spiritually, that will make life for your group richer and more productive."

As First Lady, she never crossed a picket line and in 1939, she refused to attend the President's birthday ball for the Infantile Paralysis Fund (polio) at a hotel in Alexandria, Virginia, because the waitresses were picketing for pay raises.

Eleanor Roosevelt held an active union card in The Newspaper Guild for a quarter of a century. When invited to speak before the AFL-CIO 1961 convention, she referred to the labor movement as "my movement."

Leaving an Imprint

Eleanor's personality and influence in the White House left an imprint on American politics which affected all people.

During the early years of the New Deal in the 1930s, it was Eleanor Roosevelt who went out to the farms, the migrant camps, the depressed American Heartland, and the slums to promise hope. She fought hard to extend the benefits of emergency relief and work opportunities to workers, particularly women.

In 1933, Eleanor suggested that a conference be called to examine who the federal government could provide work opportunities for unemployed artists, musicians, and writers. Out of this meeting came the forerunner of the Works Progress Administration (WPA). In 1935, the WPA was set up and it provided some of the finest cultural opportunities of the period.

Throughout her career, Eleanor Roosevelt championed the cause of human rights. Through her efforts, the issues of Black civil rights and equal opportunity in employment, the defense industries, and the armed services were given a hearing in the White House.

Demonstrating her personal commitment to civil rights at a 1939 conference on human welfare in Birmingham, Alabama, she refused to abide by the segregated seating plan. Instead, she placed her chair, for all to see, in the aisle, so she could sit half in the white section and half in the Black section.

Perhaps the most famous incident of her career occurred in that same year when the Daughters of the American Revolution (DAR) denied the great Black singer Marian Anderson permission to perform in Constitution Hall. Eleanor resigned from the DAR and then arranged for a performance at the Lincoln Memorial which 75,000 attended.

At the end of the Second Word War, Eleanor set about to insure the peace. She was one of America's delegates to the founding conference of the United Nations and was instrumental in the adoption of a declaration of human rights. Known as the "First Lady of the World," she continued her quest for world peace until her death in 1962.

Eva Perón: Out of Poverty and into Activism

Michael Neill and Laura Sanderson Healy

Eva Duarte Perón was a poor girl who rose to power and used it to redistribute the wealth of Argentina. A calculating political advocate for social aid, health reform, and charity, Perón spent her public years as wife of Argentinean dictator Juan Perón. She championed causes that would improve life in the slums that she had grown up in as a child.

In the following article, Michael Neill and Laura Sanderson Healy, writers for *People* magazine, chronicle the life of Perón, better known as Evita.

❦ ❦ ❦

O n Sept. 23, 1971, in the iron Gate suburb of Madrid, a van delivered a black wooden coffin to the mansion where Juan Peron, Argentina's exiled dictator, lived in bitter exile with Isabel, his third wife. In it lay the body of his second wife, Eva Duarte Peron. Missing for almost two decades but perfectly preserved, the embalmed corpse had been spirited out of Argentina by the generals who had ousted Peron and buried [the body] anonymously in an Italian grave. Now the generals had returned the body to Peron. He had Evita's coffin set up on the dining table. As Peron plotted his return to power, Isabel lovingly combed her predecessor's long blond hair.

Thus it is with Eva Peron: The stories that have attached themselves to her name—the true stories, like the one above, and the baroque fantasies composed by friend and enemy alike—all have the feel of a dreamlike narrative in which truth and myth are combined. In most tellings, the Evita saga hews to one of two principal themes: She was either a saint who loved the common people—or a calculating whore who slept her way to power and exploited everyone she met. . . .

Her Story

To tell Eva's story involves sifting through mounds of propaganda—much of it generated by Evita herself. In her ghostwritten 1952 autobiography, she said she had been born in Junin, a town on the Pampas, in 1922. In fact, she was born three years earlier in Los Toldos, a desolate little village in Buenos Aires Province, one of five children of Don Juan Duarte, a married rancher, and his mistress, Juana Ibarguren. A cook and seamstress, Juana had been traded to Duarte by her mother, according to family legend, for a horse and carriage.

After the death of Don Juan in 1926, Juana and her children moved to Junin, the town Evita would later claim as her birthplace, where Juana ran a boardinghouse for the town's bachelor gentlemen. Evita, the dreamer, the budding actress who haunted the local movie theater and idolized Norma Shearer, set her sights higher. She told her sister Erminda that she would marry only a prince or a president.

As a teenager, Evita, with a friend, was sexually assaulted by two young aristocrats, landowners' sons, who left the girls naked on the side of the road, to be rescued by a trucker. The tale goes far, say her supporters, in explaining why Evita became a sworn enemy of Argentina's wealthy and a champion of the poor.

When she was 15, Evita left Junin forever. Here the stories diverge, depending on the teller's politics. One version says she traveled to Buenos Aires with her mother to audition for a radio soap opera. The other maintains that she went to the dressing room of a touring tango singer, gave herself to him and then accompanied him to Buenos Aires, where she led a life of casual debauchery and calculated ambition.

Evita didn't exactly take the big city by storm—at first. Uneducated and unpolished, she wasn't a great beauty. "Her only assets," writes Alicia Dujovne Ortiz in *Eva Peron*, her 1995 biography, "Were her transparent skin and her vivid eyes." But she persisted, and over the next 10 years gradually forged a career as an actress onstage, on the radio and in the movies. According to the rumors that were spread about her after she attained power, she used the bedroom ruthlessly to get what she wanted.

Power to Avenge

By the time she met Juan Peron in 1943, she was, at 24, a well-known radio actress and a celebrity in her own right. Peron was a 48-year-old widower, a career army officer and an admirer of Fascism, which he had seen firsthand during officer training in Italy in the 1930s. After another in the dreary round of military coups that mark Argentine history, he was named Minister for Labor. He and Evita met at a festival for earthquake victims. "She literally elbowed her way through the crowd to be able to meet him and sit next to him," says Ortiz.

A Powerful Political Force

Journalism intern Amber Becker discusses how Eva Perón changed the lives of the poor in Argentina. Remembered as a saint in her homeland, Perón created the Eva Perón Foundation, a charity to provide for the needs of the downtrodden. She was instrumental in facilitating wage increases and laws to improve working conditions and successfully lobbied for passage of a bill giving women the right to vote.

When her husband became vice president in January, 1945, Evita convinced him to champion the working class by increasing their salaries. Soon after, she first tasted the thrill of political power. Evita rallied 200,000 *descamisados* ["Shirtless ones," or poor,] to demand that her husband be made president, and they succeeded. Evita's charisma and charm added to her husband's popularity.

The climb to political success was not easy for the Peróns, but Evita wouldn't let anything get in their way. She used any means necessary to make sure they succeeded, even kicking those who opposed them out of Argentina. And when the Sociedad de Beneficencia, an organization for the poor, refused to make her their

Evita became Peron's mistress, and in 1945, the year before he was elected president, they were married. "Through Peron," says Tomás Eloy Martínez, an Argentine journalist and author whose 1996 novel *Santa Evita* traces the strange journey of Evita's corpse, "Evita acquired self-confidence; he granted her legitimacy, being a military man marrying a woman who was both an actress and of bad reputation and illegitimate. When she realized how much power there was, she wanted to use that power to avenge the humiliations she had suffered."

Peron, calculating but almost devoid of personality, unleashed Evita on a dazzled nation, and for five years

honorary president, she cut their funding and used the money to create The Eva Perón Foundation. Her new charity provided clothing, shoes, food, and healthcare to the poor, and built houses for their families. Those houses became Evita's pride and joy; she named them Evita City.

While the *descamisados'* lives improved, so did Evita's. She loved living in excess: buying expensive dresses, furs, and loads of jewelry. She explained her excesses as a sign of loyalty to Argentina and rallied the people by saying, "I was once like you, but look at me now."

As her husband guided Argentina, Evita broke the rules for women at that time. She was a political force all her own. In 1947, she succeeded in getting a bill passed, giving women the right to vote. She also created the Perónista Feminist Party.

She began as the Labor Secretary for her husband, but before she could run for vice president alongside him, she became ill with uterine cancer. On May 1, 1952, Evita made her last speech and on July 26, 1952, she died.

Amber Becker, "Argentina Diva," *New Moon*, July/August 2002, p. 40.

she blazed like a meteor. As the only person Peron trusted completely, Eva, who held no office of her own, served as his political hatchet person, driving out high officials he wanted to oust. She was also his link to the masses. The poor people of Argentina—the *descamisados*, or shirtless ones—embraced her as one of their own.

To Evita, charity was a personal thing. It wasn't enough that she administered millions of dollars in health and welfare benefits through the Social Aid Foundation, which she founded after the wealthy women of Buenos Aires blackballed her from the country's foremost charity. She also visited lepers, harangued the rich and opened her doors to the poor, giving away sewing machines, bridal gowns, false teeth or whatever might be needed. Women supplicants, no matter how disheveled, were greeted with a kiss. A man who worked with her told of throwing himself between Evita and a woman with a syphilitic sore on her mouth. Evita insisted on kissing the woman "Never do that again," she told the man afterward. "It's the price I have to pay." Under Peron, and with Eva's advocacy, Argentine women got the vote for the first time in 1950.

This was the Evita of legend—the poor girl who redistributed the nation's wealth from the rich to the downtrodden. The legend does not, of course, detail the wealth the Perons distributed to themselves. With Argentina running trade surpluses achieved through beef and grain shipments during World War II, the Perons systematically looted the treasury. Evita stocked her wardrobes, jewelry cases and a Swiss bank account. As corruption and mismanagement and Juan Peron's political strong-arm tactics triggered an economic slump that would last 30 years, Evita used her considerable power over the police, the unions and the press to cow and punish her opponents.

Always frail, Evita underwent an emergency appendectomy in 1950. By some accounts, her surgeon later said that she refused to submit to a life-saving hysterectomy after tests revealed she had uterine cancer, claiming the surgery would have interrupted her work.

Evita's final appearance was at Juan Peron's second inauguration on June 4, 1952. Filled with painkillers and weighing about 80 pounds, she rode in an open car, held up by a plaster support under a long fur coat. She died seven weeks later at 33.

Mary Robinson

Nance Lucas

As a human rights attorney, Mary Robinson fought for gender equality. When Robinson was elected president of Ireland, she used her position to bring attention to global threats of war and famine. In 1997 she became the human rights commissioner for the United Nations. In the following interview with Nance Lucas, a professor at the University of Maryland, Robinson discusses her personal agenda as a forceful advocate of human rights. Robinson told Lucas that her role as head of the UN Commission on Human Rights would be as a catalyst for change. Robinson spent her five years in office as an outspoken voice for victims of human rights violations. She also reinforced relationships with the UN and nongovernmental organizations to integrate greater support for human rights issues.

❧ ❧ ❧

Mary Robinson became High Commissioner for Human Rights on September 12, 1997, following her nomination to the post by United Nations Secretary-General Kofi Annan and the endorsement of the General Assembly. Mrs. Robinson was the first woman president of Ireland (1990–1997) and member of Ireland's Upper House of Parliament for 20 years (1969–89).

Nance Lucas, "An Interview with Mary Robinson, Former President of Ireland," *Journal of Leadership & Organizational Studies*, Winter 2003. Copyright © 2003 by Baker College—Center for Graduate Studies. Reproduced by permission.

As High Commissioner, Mrs. Robinson has given priority to implementing the reform proposal of Secretary-General Kofi Annan to integrate human rights concerns in all the activities of the United Nations. In September 1998, she was the first High Commissioner to visit China, signing an agreement that should lead to a wide-ranging program of cooperation for the improvement of human rights in that country. Mrs. Robinson has also strengthened human rights monitoring in such conflict areas as Kosovo, in the Federal Republic of Yugoslavia. Her Office now has staff monitoring human rights or providing technical assistance in over 20 countries.

Mrs. Robinson came to the United Nations after a distinguished seven-year tenure as President of Ireland. As President, Mrs. Robinson developed a new sense of Ireland's economic, political and cultural links with other countries and cultures. She placed special emphasis during her Presidency on the needs of developing countries, linking the history of the Great Irish Famine to today's nutrition, poverty and policy issues, thus creating a bridge of partnership between developed and developing countries.

Mrs. Robinson was the first Head of State to visit Rwanda in the aftermath of the 1994 genocide there. She was also the first Head of State to visit Somalia following the crisis there in 1992, receiving the CARE Humanitarian Award in recognition of her efforts for that country.

Before her election as President in 1990, Mrs. Robinson served as Senator, holding that office for 20 years. In 1969 she became the youngest Reid Professor of Constitutional Law at Trinity College, Dublin. She was called to the bar in 1967, becoming a Senior Counsel in 1980, and a member of the English Bar (Middle Temple) in 1973. Educated at Trinity College, Mrs. Robinson also holds law degrees from the King's Inns in Dublin and from Harvard University. . . .

NANCE LUCAS: What do you see as the major human rights challenges facing our world today?

MARY ROBINSON: The most serious is to implement the human rights commitments that governments have made. I find it very disturbing that governments which have signed up to legal commitments somehow don't tell their finance ministers, don't tell their trade ministers in the WTO [World Trade Organization], and don't see that this is important when they're examining responsibility on the board of the World Bank. As well as implementing these commitments in their own countries, western countries should also be ensuring that they're addressing the issues of developing countries and that they're empowering them to fulfill these commitments. That's one issue and the other is the shadow of post 9/11 and the context of a language of war on terrorism, which concerns me.

NANCE LUCAS: How can ordinary global citizens facilitate systemic change to advance a human rights agenda?

MARY ROBINSON: By informing themselves of the commitments that their governments have entered into either internationally through the U.N. system or regionally. They need to use these commitments as tools of democracy side-by-side with voting to elect and to pin leaders to these responsibilities. These are effective legal tools to hold public officials accountable for the legal commitments the governments have made so we need literate civil societies in the broadest sense—women's groups, church groups, trade unions, business leaders, youth, and NGOs [nongovernmental organizations]. We need teachers to integrate human rights in the curriculum in schools and in youth clubs.

NANCE LUCAS: Part of our problem is that there is a perceived mistrust from past years of failed attempts by leaders to advance a human rights agenda. Is there a place that you know of in the world where a grassroots campaign for human rights is making a difference?

MARY ROBINSON: I see literally hundreds of examples of this. It happens in developed countries and in developing countries. I understand that there are more cultural problems in the United States because the U.S. hasn't, in fact, ratified three of the key instruments: the convention on the rights of the child, the convention for the elimination of discrimination against women, and the international covenant on economic, social, and culture rights. So this debate is not as practical for legislators or for advancing the civil society in this country. But, for example, in 191 countries in the world, the convention on the rights of the child has been ratified and therefore they're committed to guaranteeing civil and political rights, and economic, social, and cultural rights to the population up to the age of 18. The problem is to implement this!

During the month of August [2003], I was in three Asian countries where that convention had been ratified, and where civil society was working on it. One of them was China. The All-China Federation for Women was telling me that they worked on the convention on the elimination of discrimination against women and the convention on the rights of the child, and on China's reporting on those conventions. Now they were going to work with China on its first report on the International Covenant on Economic, Social and Cultural Rights. This enabled them to address poverty issues where there was discrimination against Western Provinces in China.

When I went to Cambodia, the NGOs there were doing exactly the same thing—working with the government of Cambodia, and if necessary, putting together a parallel report. Then I went to East Timor where the new government had taken office in May. For the first time people in East Timor had their own government. The NGOs there were having to adjust to finding the tools to work with the new government instead of viewing the law and government as being oppressive. They were learning that useful tools would stem from the government ratifying all six of the human rights instruments, which it has done, and then reporting over the next year or so on their status. This would be a way of addressing issues of women, children, poverty, and civil rights, etc. In Latin America, when Brazil didn't produce its report on the covenant on economic, social, and cultural rights, a rainbow-wide association of civil society groups produced an alternative report and shamed their government to do the right thing. So it's happening all over the world already.

NANCE LUCAS: Those are powerful examples but we don't know enough about them. Part of the problem is that we aren't highlighting some of the positive things that are happening as you just mentioned.

MARY ROBINSON: That is one goal that I'd like to accomplish with my Ethical Globalization Initiative—to make these examples better known so that we can use these good practices to encourage other civil society groups.

NANCE LUCAS: You are a powerful role model for other women around the world. How can we advance the leadership of women and increase the number of women leaders in all sectors?

MARY ROBINSON: I think role modeling and networking helps. For example, African women are a very powerful force in so many African countries, but they're not represented at head of state level and they weren't represented on the Secretariat of the Organization of African Unity. Now there is a commitment to change this in the ten member commission for the new

African Union, which will be voted on [in 2003] and take office at the next meeting of the African Union. In the constitution of the African Union there's a provision that half of the commission members will be women, two members, one of which will be a woman will be put forward from each of the five regions in Africa. If that happens, it will have a dramatic impact on women's rights in Africa because at the level of the body running the African Union, half of them will be women. I'm not saying that they have to all be great women. They will be a mixture like the men. But the women leaders most likely will align their leadership with the values of civil society.

There's a good deal of networking of women's groups throughout the different regions of the world, and now they're networking with each other. They're also realizing the importance of resources. For example, I'm very supportive of the Global Fund for Women. I spoke recently at their 15th anniversary because they fund small women's self-development projects internationally. This is seed money for very valuable women's work.

All of these things are important and so are role models. I like to refer to Eleanor Roosevelt, a great American human rights person. I think Eleanor is important because the United States should look back to her extraordinary leadership in advancing human rights in chairing the Commission on Human Rights that drafted the Universal Declaration of Human Rights. She is one of the great heroines of human rights. If we could rekindle her spirit in the United States, that would be very good for human rights all around the world.

NANCE LUCAS: How did Eleanor Roosevelt influence your own leadership?

MARY ROBINSON: I was very impressed by her straightforward, practical approach. When she was Chair of the

Commission, she was working with very eminent legal scholars—a Chinese scholar, a Lebanese scholar, Rene Cassin of France, and John Humphries of Canada. She emphasized the importance of ensuring that the Universal Declaration would be written in simple straightforward language, not in lawyer language or U.N. speak. She said that if I can't understand it, how is it going to be understood in small places close to home where human rights must matter.

Secondly, she fought with the State Department at the time and insisted that the Universal Declaration must encompass not just civil and political rights such as a right to a fair trial, freedom of religion, and freedom from torture, but also the right to food, to safe water, to health, and to education. This was essential for the integrity of human rights. That was incredible leadership in her time. She also tried to mobilize public opinion through her writing as a journalist and as an opinion former. We have the roles and now the challenge is to implement them. So her approach is highly relevant in getting civil society groups to hold governments accountable for the legal commitments they've made.

NANCE LUCAS: What was the single greatest risk you've taken as a leader and what lessons did you learn?

MARY ROBINSON: I think it was a risk to take on the job of U.N. High Commissioner for Human Rights, because it was extremely difficult. I was warned that it was under resourced. I was warned that it wasn't prestigious. I was warned that human rights were very poisonous at the international level. I had other possible offers that were, on paper anyway, more important, larger, and safer. So, I suppose that was, in a way, the greatest challenge.

NANCE LUCAS: How do we reverse the egregious crimes against humanity we see increasing all over the world? And, what advice would you give the world's leaders today in their efforts to confront terrorism?

MARY ROBINSON: Certainly, the experience of giving leadership at the U.N. level on human rights and wanting to be a voice for the victims and therefore trying to be close to those who suffer from violations of human rights was a very telling experience because the extent

Increasing the Visibility of Human Rights

Aisha Labi discusses how Mary Robinson's tenure as UN high commissioner for human rights brought attention to human rights and increased the role of nongovernmental and regional organizations for this cause. Labi is a writer for the magazine Time International*'s European division.*

Two years into her tenure as the United Nations' High Commissioner for Human Rights, Mary Robinson is reevaluating herself. Having spent much of her career championing the cause of Irish national identity within Europe, she now finds these categorizations somewhat limiting. "I spend most of my time both thinking about and identifying with much less privileged regions of the world," she explains. "I'm Irish and European, but now a citizen of the world in the true sense."

Since her appointment as the U.N. High Commissioner for Human Rights, Robinson has been a relentless advocate for the most vulnerable of her fellow citizens. With the same forthrightness that helped her imbue with authority the largely ceremonial role of President of the Irish Republic, she has remade the U.N. job in her own image. While human rights advocates have often focused on abuses by unfriendly regimes, Robinson has taken an unstintingly democratic approach. During NATO's [the North Atlantic Treaty Organization's] bombing of Yugoslavia, she questioned the operation's legality and crit-

of the violations of human rights was very shocking to me. The extent of torture by police because they simply aren't trained to gather evidence is a fact of life in so many countries. The police regularly torture and regularly use violence, and in many cases when women come to them to complain that they've been raped,

icized the civilian casualties resulting from the air campaign. "When you say that what you're doing is for humanitarian reasons, you must be careful not to make significantly worse the humanitarian situation of a high proportion of citizens," she cautions. Yet she was also unyielding in her condemnation of the "vicious abuses" of [Yugoslav dictator Slobodan] Milosevic and his troops.

And it is not just the headline-making causes that Robinson espouses. She has called for the overall conception of human rights to be broadened, with more attention paid to social, cultural and economic rights. Another theme she stresses is the increasingly important role of non-governmental and regional organizations. In Serbia, for example, where "people are starved of contact and support to help them build a society of human rights," she points to the importance of the Organization for Security and Cooperation in Europe in normalizing society.

Robinson's advocacy has turned her post into one of the U.N.'s most visible. She has even been mooted as a possible successor to Kofi Annan as Secretary-General—not an unreasonable prediction given her track record. In 1990 she was elected Ireland's first woman President. By the time she left office a few months shy of the end of her term to take up the U.N. job, her approval ratings had soared and she had won international plaudits.

Aisha Labi, "Mary Robinson: Humanitarian, 55," *Time International*, September 13, 1999, p. 36.

they'll be raped in the prison station. That was one powerful lesson.

The fact that globalizing factors are worsening situations for many victims of violations is disturbing. For example, the rapid growth in the trafficking of human beings, women and children. This is an appalling factor of modern globalization. It's also a factor of poverty. If a country in transition, like countries in the former Soviet Union, falls into greater economic difficulty, then you can see the graph immediately of the rise in the women and girls that will be trafficked. The same thing happens in Asia. When an Asian country dips in its economy, it is women and children who will be trafficked as human persons. That trafficking very often links with other trafficking in drugs and arms. The degree of criminality is truly frightening.

We have to recognize that one of the ways of describing globalization is that it is a privatization of power. Governments have less power and are tending to assume less responsibility to deal with some of these issues. So I come to your second question. How should government deal with addressing the issue of terrorism? I certainly am concerned that since the terrible attacks in the United States on 9/11, the approach has tended to be to promote a war on terrorism and there must be a coalition to fight that war. I was very concerned at the time to apply a human rights analysis to those attacks. I sat with my colleagues and we concluded based on the existing jurisprudence that the attacks were undoubtedly crimes against humanity. Therefore, there was an obligation under International Human Rights Law for every country to cooperate in bringing the perpetrators of the crimes to justice.

I like this approach because it characterizes those who committed those atrocious acts of violence as the worst criminals. You cannot, in the name of any religion, invoke that religion to commit a crime against humanity. So, you isolate them in that way from the religion that they were claiming to act in the name of. I think that's extremely important to prevent a kind of war between religions or between civilizations. If you adopt the approach of a war on terrorism, there is at least some risk that you in fact give a standing to the terrorists: that it's a war, and that those on the other side can start using the language of war against the great Satan, or the language that we're freedom fighters, or whatever. This is really very troubling because in some parts of the world, this is happening. You have millions of young people who are frustrated, despairing, unemployed, and now they're getting an excitement of a war against a stronger, but in their views, a very bad aggressor. It shows that this situation can be manipulated in this way. Whereas if the focus of every country was on bringing perpetrators of terrible crimes to justice and if we understood the importance of institutions like the International Criminal Court to end impunity and to say to bullies and perpetrators of gross violations you may run, but you can not hide—we'll get you eventually—I believe we would be more effective.

The impact of the Pinochet Ruling of the House of Lords on Latin American countries means that gross violators of human rights can no longer go comfortably for medical treatment to other countries. They can no longer be secure that when they travel to countries, they won't be arrested and brought to trial before countries that are prepared to exercise extraterritorial jurisdiction. It would be much more effective if we had international court jurisdiction to complement national court jurisdiction. So it's an irony at the moment that despite the rightful emphasis on trying to bring those who commit terrorist acts to justice—and I'm unequivocally in favor of that because acts of terrorism are totally contrary to human rights—there is not, in fact, a United States commitment to reinforce the International Criminal Court which is now beginning its work in the Hague. It's an extremely important advance and it should be fully supported. It should apply to everyone without exception.

NANCE LUCAS: Given this publication's theme on leadership in diverse societies, do you believe that we have more in common across boundaries and borders than not? Do we have more values in common than not?

MARY ROBINSON: I think we have more in common than not around the world because our hopes and aspirations are very alike. Also, I think we're now in a situation where all countries are becoming more diverse and therefore it is incumbent on leaders to learn to value diversity and to see it as an enrichment and to practice it at every level. It is one of the lessons that we tried to drive home in the preparations for the very difficult world conference against racism in Durban. The text that was finally, with great difficulty, agreed upon at the official level is actually a good text. That's not understood in America because when the United States and Israel left the meeting, it was assumed that the conference must have failed, but actually the conference succeeded against the odds. Unfortunately three days after it succeeded we had the attacks of 9/11 and that kind of wiped the outcome of the conference off the agenda.

It does provide the world with a modern agenda to value diversity, to totally combat all forms of racism, xenophobia, anti-Semitism, anti-Arab, and anti-Islamic sentiments. Unfortunately, each of those is rising. Anti-Semitism is rising very seriously in countries in Europe. It preoccupied me in my last months as High Commissioner in figuring out how to address this and how to prevent this terrible racism from seeping up again in a very evil way. Since 9/11, we live in a climate of fear and we need to combat fears becoming reasons for racial profiling and all the things we're seeing—the harshness now against refugees and asylum seekers. I think that the focus on diversity, on being enriched by diversity, by having businesses highlight the value of diversity in the workplace, having local leaders highlight and preventing any discrimination against those of a different color, those of a different eye shape, or whatever is vital to sustaining peaceful and civil societies.

Profiles . in . History

Exposing Human Rights Abuses

Tenzin Gyatso: The Dalai Lama of Tibet

Pico Iyer

Tenzin Gyatso is the current Dalai Lama of Tibet. Although the Dalai Lama is invested with the powers of a king and is considered to be the spiritual leader of 6 million Tibetans, Gyatso has been ruling his countrymen in exile since 1959. Gyatso spent eight years trying to resist Chinese ruler Mao Tse-tung's military advancement into Tibet until he feared that his death would lead to the slaughter of his people. Gyatso fled to India, where for the last forty years he has peacefully protested what he terms China's "cultural genocide." As a result of his efforts, the Dalai Lama received the 1989 Nobel Peace Prize. In the following selection, Pico Iyer, a well-known writer on international culture, recounts the Dalai Lama's turbulent life and describes his current role as a spokesperson for the rights of Tibetans. Iyer points out that although Gyatso has attained celebrity status among followers in the West and is highly revered as a religious figure, he considers himself first and foremost a Buddhist monk.

Pico Iyer, "The God in Exile," *Time*, vol. 150, December 22, 1997, p. 72. Copyright © 1997 by Time, Inc. All rights reserved. Reproduced by permission.

Windows are broken and paths half paved in the ramshackle little town of Dharamsala, India, where the Dalai Lama lives. The absolute spiritual and temporal ruler of Tibet still has to drive 10 hours over roads crazy with scooters and cows every time he needs to take a flight (from New Delhi, 300 miles to the south). And when you call his tiny office, you usually hear that "all circuits are busy"—or the five-digit number changed yesterday, or, amid a blizzard of static, you get cut off in mid-sentence, the only small consolation being that you are put on hold to the tune of London Bridge Is Falling Down.

Yet to this makeshift exile center come moviemakers, camera crews and seekers from around the world, and from it, in the months before I returned to see him, the Dalai Lama had visited all five major continents, in his near desperate attempt to save occupied Tibet before it dies.

His predicament, in fact, is one for which I can think of no precedent or parallel. Trained for 18 years in the intricacies of Tibetan Buddhist metaphysics, one of the most accomplished philosophers in his tradition has spent most of the past half-century entangled in geopolitics, trying to protect and rescue his homeland from the Chinese forces that attacked in 1950 and drove him into exile nine years later. His cause is not made easier by the fact that much of the world is trying to court China, the world's largest marketplace, and that he is the guest of a huge nation with problems of its own that would rather he kept quiet. And, as church and state incarnate, the Dalai Lama, winner of the 1989 Nobel Prize for Peace, finds himself denied the privileges of a full-fledged political leader even as he cannot enjoy the peaceful immunity of a purely religious figure.

The ever pragmatic Tibetan has responded to this

predicament by taking his cause directly to the world, traveling almost constantly (on a refugee's yellow "identity certificate"), answering questions in 20,000-seat pop-concert halls about everything from [assisted-suicide proponent doctor] Jack Kevorkian to TV violence, and letting his speeches be broadcast live on the floor of London dance clubs. This has led to the unlikely sight of a "simple monk" (as he always calls himself)—born and raised in a culture that had scarcely seen a Westerner when the [twentieth] century began—now seeming as visible, and even as fashionable, a figure as [film actor] Richard Gere, [comic actor] John Cleese speaks for him in London, [photographer] Henri Cartier-Bresson records his teachings around France, Adam Yauch of the Beastie Boys interviews him in Rome for *Rolling Stone*. In the past few years he has opened 11 Offices of Tibet, everywhere from Canberra to Moscow, and last year [1996] alone provided prefaces and forewords for roughly 30 books. The 14th Dalai Lama is surely the only Ocean of Wisdom, Holder of the White Lotus and Protector of the Land of Snows to serve as guest editor of *French Vogue*.

At the time I revisited him, the Dalai Lama was contemplating the latest strange turn in this enforced interaction with the modern world: the $70 million Hollywood movie *Seven Years in Tibet* and Martin Scorsese's remarkable new film, *Kundun*, both of which tell the story of his early life. Sitting cross-legged in his armchair, rocking back and forth as he spoke and always keeping an eye out to make sure my cup of tea was full, the famously accessible doctor of metaphysics talked with full-bodied candor, for day after day, about his death, the increasingly public divisions within the Tibetan community and the new pressures of his spotlighted life. Accepting donations from Shoko Asahara, the head of the Aum Shinrikyo group in Japan that later allegedly planted deadly sarin gas in the subways of Tokyo, was, he says frankly, "a mistake. Due to ignorance. So this proves"—a mischievous gleam escapes— "I'm not a living Buddha!" He'd love to delegate some responsibilities to his deputies, he confesses, but "even if some of my Cabinet ministers wanted to give public talks, nobody would come." And the single most difficult thing in his life, he admits, is "meeting with politicians. Realistically speaking, it's just symbolic. They cannot do much." Yet, as Helen Tworkov, editor in chief of the New York Buddhist magazine *Tricycle*, puts it, the simple, paradoxical fact is that "he needs people with money, he needs people with power, he needs people with influence."

And so the man who would clearly be happier just meditating finds himself turning to Democrats and Republicans, instructing 140,000 exiled Tibetans in the ways of the world, and winning all the admiration and attention he doesn't particularly need, while making scant headway in his cause. Last September [1997] some reporters openly criticized the (non-Tibetan) organizers of his trip to Australia because of their $20 T shirts and official sponsorship from Nike, Thai International Airlines and Ford. I must confess, though, that I know of this only because the Dalai Lama told me of it—and a caustic clipping about the "Dalai Lama Show," the only item up on the bulletin board of the Dolma Ling Nunnery in Dharamsala.

To appreciate fully the incongruities of Tenzin Gyatso's life in the celebrity age, you have to recall that he was born in a cowshed in a tiny farming village in what was locally known as the Wood Hog Year (1935). The previous Dalai Lama, the 13th, had been one of the great reforming spirits of a tradition whose leaders had all too often been ineffectual boys manipulated by regents. Beset by imperialists of all stripes, the farsighted

Lama, in his last written testament, predicted a time in Tibet's history, soon, when "monks and monasteries will be destroyed . . . [and] all beings will be sunk in great hardship and overwhelming fear."

Upon his death, the senior monks of Lhasa set about finding his successor in the traditional fashion. The regent went to the sacred lake of Lhamoi Lhatso, famous for its visions, and saw in its waters an image of a gold-roofed, three-story monastery beside a winding path. Other signs appeared. The embalmed body of the departed ruler seemed to move from pointing south to pointing toward the northeast. And auspicious cloud formations also appeared in the northeast. When a search party of monks arrived at the 20-family settlement of Takster, in the northeastern province of Amdo, its members were startled to find a gold-roofed, three-story monastery beside a winding path. They were even more taken aback when a two-year-old boy greeted them with familiarity and addressed their leader, disguised as a servant, by the name of his temple in distant Lhasa. The mischievous toddler, who slept in the kitchen of a mud-and-stone house, would become the 14th Dalai Lama.

At the age of four he was installed upon the Lion Throne in Lhasa and inducted into a formidable course of monastic studies. By the age of six he was choosing his own regent, and by the time he was 11 he was weathering a civil uprising. The Dalai Lama has written with typical warmth about his unworldly boyhood in the cold, dark, thousand-room Potala Palace, playing games with the palace sweepers, rigging up a hand-cranked projector on which he could watch Tarzan movies and *Henry V*, and clobbering his only real play-mate—his immediate elder brother Lobsang Samten—serene in the knowledge that no one would readily punish a boy regarded as the incarnation of the god of compassion. Yet the dominant characteristic of his childhood was its loneliness. Often, he recalls, he would go onto the rooftop of his palace and watch the other boys of Lhasa playing in the streets. And each time his brother left, he remembers "standing at the window, watching, my heart full of sorrow as he disappeared into the distance."

Tibet itself (with an army of just 8,500) was in an equally vulnerable state of remoteness when Chinese forces, newly united by Mao Zedong, attacked its eastern frontiers in 1950. Hurriedly, on the advice of the State Oracle (who delivered counsel while in a trance), the 15-year-old boy was invested with full political authority, and while still in his teens, he traveled to Beijing in 1954, against the wishes of his protective people, to negotiate face to face with Mao.

Five years later, when angry Tibetans rose up ever more fiercely against Chinese aggression, their young leader consulted the State Oracle again and, one night, dressed as a humble soldier, slipped out of his summer palace, with his family and some bodyguards. For two weeks the party traveled over the highest mountains on earth, dodging Chinese planes and moving only under the cover of darkness, until at last, suffering from dysentery and on the back of a hybrid yak, the Dalai Lama arrived in India and began a new life in exile.

That parting lives within him still, and when I asked him last year [1996] about the saddest moment of his life, he looked into the distance and recalled how "I left the Norbulingka Palace that late night, and some of my close friends, and one dog I left behind. Then, just when I was crossing the border into India, I remember my final farewell, mainly to my bodyguards. They were deliberately facing toward the Chinese, and when they bade farewell, they were determined to return. So that means"—his eyes are close to misting over—"they were facing death or something like that." Since then, he has never seen the land he was born to rule.

By now everyone knows of the luminous charisma of the friendly philosopher, intensified, friends say, by the long retreats he enjoyed while the world had no interest in him. His particular strength lies in his ability to make one-on-one contact even in the most crowded and impersonal of settings. "I don't like to play artificial," he tells me. "I really feel it's wasteful." In recent years his English has grown notably more fluent, and eight years of post-Nobel interviews mean that he can now tell television crews where to set up their cameras. The Dalai Lama may not be less jolly than before, but he is, I think, more determined to speak from the serious side of himself; and where he used to greet me with an Indian namaste [a respectful bow with the palms pressed together at the chest], he shakes my hand now—though it's still the case that he doesn't so much shake your hand as rub it within his own as if to impart to it some of his warmth.

Now and then, as we talk, he takes off his glasses and rubs his eyes, and close aides say that recently, for the first time, they've seen him slumped back in his chair, exhausted. He still arises every morning at 3:30, he says matter-of-factly, and every day recites four hours of scriptures (while taking walks, praying for the Chinese and riding his exercise bike). "I still love flowers," he says, "and occasionally do some repair work, of watches and small instruments." But mostly the only breaks he can take regularly are to listen to the BBC World Service. "I am addicted," he confesses happily.

Yet his biggest problem may still be simple isolation. Most Tibetans, after all, continue to regard him quite literally as a god, to the point where even fluent English speakers are too intimidated to serve as his translators. He works with a painfully inexperienced staff drawn from an exile population smaller than that of Peoria, Ill.

(two generations of whom have never even seen Tibet). And as fast as the Dalai Lama tries to push democracy on his people, they try to press autocracy on him, leading to an ungainly tug-of-war in which most Tibetans are unswervingly obedient to the Dalai Lama in every matter except that of the Dalai Lama's fallibility.

In that context he must operate alone and rely on a few trusted friends and relatives, such as his younger brother Tendzin Choegyal, who lives down the road in Dharamsala and speaks his mind with fearless rigor. Thus, while the Dalai Lama officially professes to be unconcerned about all the complications that have arisen as Tibet and Tibetan Buddhism have suddenly spread around the world, his brother openly calls it "a hell of a hodgepodge" and notes that too many lamas take advantage of their impressionable Western admirers, who, in search of instant enlightenment, are prey to what he calls "the Shangri-La syndrome."

This is a particularly vexed matter because Tibetan Buddhism is an unusually charged and esoteric set of practices uncommonly difficult to translate, "a unique blend," as the Buddhist scholar Christmas Humphreys once wrote, "of the noblest Buddhist principles and debased sorcery." Its core, as with all Buddhism, is a belief in suffering and emptiness, and the need for compassion in the face of those. But unlike the stripped-down austerities of Zen, say, Tibetan Buddhism swarms with animist spirits, vivid symbolic depictions of copulating bodies, and Tantric practices of magic and sexuality that, taken out of context or practiced without the right training, are inflammable.

The Dalai Lama's very refusal to be dictatorial and his calm assurance that Tibetan Buddhist centers, unlike their Roman Catholic counterparts, "have no central authority" and are "all quite independent" have left him somewhat powerless as all kinds of questionable things are done in the name of his philosophy (a prominent lama was slapped with a $10 million sexual-harassment suit in California). And his wish to make peace among the four main schools of Tibetan Buddhism has so infuriated a few that earlier this year [1997] three members of his inner circle were found murdered in their beds, apparently by a breakaway sect.

Though the Dalai Lama deals with such problems serenely, having endured insurrections for a half-century, the issues of delegating responsibility and authorizing the reincarnations of departed lamas take on particular urgency as he passes through his 60s. The finding of a new Dalai Lama when all Tibet is in Chinese hands would in the best of circumstances be treacherous; but it became doubly so two years ago [in 1995], when Beijing unilaterally hijacked the second highest incarnation in Tibet, that of the Panchen Lama, by placing the Dalai Lama's six-year-old choice under house arrest and installing a candidate of its own. (The Panchen Lama is the figure officially responsible for authorizing the Dalai Lama's own incarnation—and the maneuver suggested that the Chinese may have few qualms about coming up with their own puppet as the next Dalai Lama.)

In response to this, the man trained for 18 years in dialectics has been canny. More than a decade ago, he reminds me, he said that "if I die in the near future, and the Tibetan people want another reincarnation, a 15th Dalai Lama, while we are still outside Tibet, my reincarnation will definitely appear outside Tibet. Because"—the logic, as ever, is rock solid—"the very purpose of the incarnation is to fulfill the work that has been started by the previous life." So, he goes on, "the reincarnation of the 14th Dalai Lama, logically, will not be a reincarnation that disturbs, or is an obstacle to, that work. Quite clear, isn't it?" In any case, he says cheerfully, "at a cer-

tain state the Dalai Lama institution will disappear. That
does not mean that Tibetan Buddhism will cease. But the
institution comes and goes, comes and goes."

As ever, few of his supporters are equally ready to acquiesce in such lese majeste. (When I ask a group of Tibetan officials if this one will be the last Dalai Lama,
they all say anxiously, "No, no.") And even relatives
have sometimes found it hard to countenance his policy of forgiving the Chinese (he once described Mao as
"remarkable," has referred to himself as "half Marxist,
half Buddhist," and has stepped back from his original
demands of independence to calling only for an au-
tonomous "Zone of Peace"). The pressure on him to
forswear his policy of nonviolence has intensified as the
years go by, and Chinese repression comes ever closer
to rendering Tibet extinct.

"In one way, yes," he tells me, "my position has become weaker, because there's been no development, no
progress. In spite of my open approach, of maximum
concessions, the Chinese position becomes even harder
and harder." Last year [1996] all photographs of the exiled leader were banned in Tibet, and monks and nuns
continue to be imprisoned and tortured at will, in what
the International Commission of Jurists long ago called
a policy of "genocide." Yet, he argues, all but banging
his fist on the arm of his chair, "to isolate China is totally wrong. China needs the outside world, and the
outside world needs China."

When I left Dharamsala at dawn, the Dalai Lama
was leading his monks in a three-hour ceremony while
the sun came up behind the distant snowcaps. It struck
me that the man has lived out a kind of archetypal destiny of our times: a boy born in a peasant village in a
world that had scarcely seen a wheel has ended up con-
fronting the great forces of the day—exile, global travel
and, especially, the mass media; and a man from a cul-

ture known as the "Forbidden Kingdom" now faces machine guns on the one hand and Chinese discos around the Potala Palace on the other. While Tibet is eroded in its homeland, it threatens to be commodified—or turned into an exotic accessory—abroad.

Yet to this state-of-the-art challenge the Dalai Lama brings, in his own words, a "radical informality," a gift for cutting through to the heart of things and an unusually open and practical mind. If I had to single out one sovereign quality in him, it would be alertness, whether he's reminding me of a sentence he delivered to me seven years before or picking out a friend's face in the middle of a jam-packed prayer hall.

This mindfulness, as Buddhists might call it, is particularly critical these days as the Dalai Lama finds himself more and more appealing to people who know nothing of his philosophy—and may even be hostile to it. The Tibetan has delivered lectures on the Gospels, celebrated the Internet as a talisman of human interdependence and, especially, mastered the art of talking to ordinary people in ordinary human terms, about "spirituality without faith." As his longtime friend the composer Philip Glass says, "He talks about compassion, he talks about right living. And it's very powerful and persuasive to people because it's clear he's not there to convert them."

The Dalai Lama is unbending on this point. "Out of 5.8 billion people in the world," he tells me, "the majority of them are certainly not believers. We can't argue with them, tell them they should be believers. No! Impossible! And, realistically speaking, if the majority of humanity remains nonbelievers, it doesn't matter. No problem! The problem is that the majority have lost, or ignore, the deeper human values—compassion, a sense of responsibility. That is our big concern. For whenever there is a community without deeper human

Harry Wu: Challenging China's Human Rights Record

Anthony C. LoBaido

Harry Wu told Anthony C. LoBaido, an international correspondent for *WorldNetDaily*, that he was falsely arrested as a counterrevolutionary and spent nineteen years in a Chinese labor camp. When he was released from prison, Wu came to America as a visiting scholar at the University of California at Berkeley, teaching during the day and living as a homeless person at night. In 1990 Wu testified before the U.S. Senate on Chinese labor camps. His documented research has encouraged U.S. customs to detain Chinese imports to the United States. In the following excerpt LoBaido details Wu's life and claims that Wu has become the only human rights activist working against the Chinese Communist political system that keeps slave-labor camps, known as the laogai, in operation.

❧ ❧ ❧

The name Harry Wu needs no introduction to freedom-loving Americans. Having survived the laogai or slave-labor gulags of communist China, Wu came to America and testified before Congress about the horrors of China's slave-labor system.

Wu was born into a bourgeois family that was fairly affluent when compared to the rest of China's population.

"My father was a banker and my mother had descended from a family of well-to-do landlords," Wu told *WorldNetDaily* [WND]. "My youth was one of peace and pleasure. Then in 1949 came the communist revolution, led by Mao [Tse-tung]. My life changed dramatically. During my teen-age years, my father lost all his properties. We had money problems. The government took over all the property in the country. We even had to sell my piano."

"At first things seemed OK in China. The government was busy with the Korean War and suppressing the old government elements. The first four to five years after the revolution we were basically OK as a nation. But then the government began to wipe out religion—Buddhists, Catholics and all Christians."

Wu said that during the initial years after the communist revolution, "the majority of the Chinese people wanted to dedicate their efforts toward serving the people of the nation. We believed this would make China a wealthy nation.

"The communist government told the people, 'There will be no more imperialism, no more colonialism.' In China at that time, the government stopped prostitution, gambling and drugs. We believed that if we worked hard, we would have a bright future. The communist leaders killed many bourgeois landlord elements and demolished the churches.

"There had been many problems in China since the

Japanese invasion [in 1937]. We believed at first that the new communist government would be clean and straight and honest. We wanted to work hard and discipline ourselves for the good of the next generation. We believed in the future of communism, and Mao was treated as a god."

But that initial euphoria did not last for Wu and his family.

"When I was 18, I went to Beijing to begin studies at the Beijing College of Geology. At that time, I realized that my parents were at the top of society, a banker and the daughter of a landlord. I began to question myself and say, 'Do I deserve this when so many are so poor?' I thought that maybe the communist revolution would be good for the whole country."

This sentiment was shared by many Chinese intellectuals of the time, including the Dalai Lama, who, in September 1999, told *Time* Magazine, "It was only when I went to China in 1954–55 that I actually studied Marxist thought. Once I understood Marxism, I even expressed my wish to become a Communist Party member. Marxism talked about self-reliance, without depending on a creator or a god. That was very attractive. I still think that if a genuine communist movement had come to Tibet, there would have been much benefit to the people."

"When I was 20, I was a sophomore and majoring in geology and engineering. I played shortstop on the baseball team and was the captain. I had a girlfriend, too," said Wu.

Little did Wu know that storm clouds were gathering on his horizon. It was to be the last "normal" era of his life for several decades.

"In 1957 came something called 'The 100 Flowers Movement.' The communists named it as such because all Chinese were supposed to 'blossom,' [no matter what their views were]. The Communist Party invited me to a meeting where I was encouraged to speak my mind. Actually, I didn't have much to say."

Wu told *WorldNetDaily* about the events that transpired at that meeting and how he had been lured into a trap by the Communist Party.

"Well, first of all, I said, 'I think the Communist Party has to correct their privileged status. The common Chinese have second- and third-class status under them.' Then I said secondly that 'the 1956 Soviet invasion of Hungary is a violation of international law.' At that time, the People's Republic of China was a supporter of the Soviet Union."

Wu told *WorldNetDaily* that he never attended any other political conferences or walked or demonstrated on the streets of Beijing.

"Then two weeks later, we had another meeting with the Communist Party branch at my university. At this meeting, they said, 'Harry Wu is a counter-revolutionary rightist. He comes from bourgeoisie. He has actively attacked the Communist Party. He is a very dangerous enemy of the Party of the People.'"

Wu added that the Communist Party had members at every university, factory, farm, school and hospital to keep an eye on the people.

Speaking of the political goal behind the 100 Flowers Movement, Wu told *WorldNetDaily*, "The CP (Communist Party) leaders' idea was, 'We have to let the snakes [anti-communists] come out—then we will destroy them.' They said that even though I had not committed a 'bad' crime, I erred by not admitting the crime. I had resisted it. Therefore, I was to receive a certain kind of punishment."

"I had 24-hour surveillance put on me. Every week, I had to write a self-examination paper and a confession. My parents, girlfriend and friends had to denounce me publicly. I felt that my future and freedom was gone. People feel I am a criminal. Nobody sympathized with me. I was one of the 550,000 purged during the 100 Flowers Movement. The actual figure of those purged is closer to 1 million."

Soon after, Wu decided that he would have to escape from China.

"At that time, I still believed in communism and that it would do good for the country. Then I realized, however, that I must escape from this country. To the CP, I had committed a very serious political crime. We had a small group of dissidents who planned to flee from China. But we were under surveillance. The communist police state found out about our plans to escape, and they caught us.

"Of course there was no trial, court or paperwork. I was sent to a slave-labor camp. The first night in the camp, they told me that I had been sentenced to life imprisonment. I was bourgeois, stubborn and had resisted. I was sentenced to a life of re-education on April 27, 1960. I was only 23 years of age."

Life in the Laogai

"According to Chinese law, all prisoners must perform labor. There was construction, railroads, iron mines, livestock, farming wheat and rice, machinery. All of these fields had forced labor. If we didn't perform any labor, the police guards would say, 'How can we help you to become a newborn person if you don't work?'"

Inside the camp, Wu told *WorldNetDaily*, the prisoners were graded on political performance and labor performance.

"We worked seven days per week and 30 days per month. Each worker had to fulfill a quota. If you did not meet the quota, they would reduce your food or send you to solitary confinement. For your political

Wu's Motivation

Journalist Carolyn Jung discusses what motivates Harry Wu to champion human rights in China.

For Hongda Harry Wu, there has been no escaping the past. It drives him, haunts him, consumes him.

The scholar and human rights champion . . . has spent the last decade working meticulously to expose human rights abuses in a Chinese labor camp system that imprisoned him for 19 years. . . .

Before he went to China to investigate the camps in 1991, he wrote in his will: "Returning to the mainland holds great dangers for me—not the least of which are the possibilities of losing once more the freedom and happiness that were so hard to come by in the first place. But the crashing sound in my ear seems to keep asking, 'Who will go?' And the answer that comes back to this question is, 'If I don't go, who else will?' . . .

Wu has said that one of his goals is to engrain the word "laogai"—"reform through labor," the slogan of the camps—into the human psyche, to make it as identifiable as the term "Holocaust" for some of the world's worst atrocities.

Over the years, he has chronicled a production system where prison labor is used in coal mines, factories and farms all over China. He has charged that more than 50 million prisoners have been forced into that system in the past 40 years and that 20 million of them have died from starvation. . . .

He is often up until 3 A.M., deciphering Chinese government documents on products and revenues to estimate how many people are imprisoned in various camps.

Carolyn Jung, "Arrested Opponent of Chinese Government Has Dedicated Life to Cause," Knight-Ridder/Tribune News Service, July 4, 1995.

performance, we had to make a confession for our crimes. A prisoner could not practice his religion. You have to betray yourself.

"At first I worked in a chemical factory in Beijing. . . . There was no protection for the slave laborers. We got burns on our skin, and many people were injured. Later, I worked at a brick factory and then in an iron mine. Later, a steel factory and then a farm. Between 1972 and 1979, I worked in a coal mine. Through all my 20 years in the slave-labor camps, I never once saw my family. My mother passed away in 1960 shortly after I was sentenced to the laogai."

Wu said that he found it difficult to resist the horrendous dehumanization of the slave-labor camps.

"I realized that I cannot resist them. I am no longer a human being. When you think of being a human being, what do you think of . . . ? You think of freedom, your future, dignity, sex, business, children. I was sentenced for life in the slave-labor camps. There was no freedom for thinking. How can you fight for those things? In the beginning, the first two years in the slave-labor camp, I tried my best to say to myself, 'I am innocent.' But you had to give up your political beliefs and your faith or you would get tortured. So you pretend. You work hard and obey, or there would be big trouble for you."

During this time, Wu became spiritually despondent.

"I had been baptized as a Catholic when I was 12-years-old. This was one of the biggest events of my early years. When I went to the laogai, I tried to remain calm. When I prayed I would say, 'Where are you God? We are human beings, and we are suffering!'"

Wu's mindset was greatly altered inside the slave-labor camps.

"Ideals like love and kindness—you don't think about these things inside the laogai. Food was a major problem. The prison guards told us, 'You will get good food for good behavior.' But we did not. We never had any eggs. Maybe some pork scraps once per month. We ate corn, soybeans and vegetable soup. Everyone in the laogai system wanted to steal food. All of the slave laborers became animals. You can take the very best men in the world, and if you put them in the laogai, after a time they will all become beasts," lamented Wu.

"I lost weight. My lowest weight was 36 kilograms [about 80 pounds]. I almost died. I was like a skeleton. My skin was thin. The bones were light."

Asked if he ever thought about trying to escape from the laogai, Wu said, "Yes, I would have been able to escape. But I thought, 'Where would I go—to my parents house? If I went there, they would have to turn me in or they themselves would be sent to a slave-labor camp.' There would be no food for me and no money. Under the Communist regime, all food is controlled. Each Chinese citizen would get monthly food coupons with strict registration procedures that were enforced. There were no restaurants where I could go and eat."

A Glimmer of Hope

Wu said that the death of Chairman Mao in 1976 was a turning point of sorts for the communist dictatorship.

"When Mao died, the communist government was in a crisis. Their car was in front of the cliff so to speak. The Communist Party realized it had to adapt. Then came Deng Xiou Ping. Deng said, 'I don't care if the cat is black or white, just as long as he can catch the mouse.' He meant that the communist government had to feed the people. Whether the system was communism or had capitalist elements was irrelevant. A cat is still a cat, be it black or white.

"The Communist Party then decided that it would release the old counter-revolutionaries. I was among them. But sadly, many others had returned to ashes. The purpose of these releases was to reduce tension. People at that time in China had no money or food, so the government realized they must pull back a little and release some prisoners."

Added Wu, "Communist ideology takes away the land, banks, factories and farms. There is no means of production that is privately owned. North Korea, the Soviet Union and her allies, and China remained communist through 1979. China had been communist since 1949. Deng Xiou Ping said that the CP would allow foreign companies to come back to China. Had he given up the communist revolution? No. The CP still had the same constitution. As I said, Deng felt, 'If we want to remain in the center of power, we need money and food to stop demonstrations by the citizens of China. Black or white, we are still a cat.'"

On the Road to Freedom

After 20 long and brutal years, Harry Wu was let out of the laogai system on Feb. 21, 1979. He was 42 years of age.

"I had spent all of my 20s and 30s in the camps. I had not had any access to movies, food, music, a girlfriend, family or a library," he told WND.

"After I was released, I got a job at a university. But the party members there reminded me, 'You are free, but you have a big tail. Wrap it between your legs.' I realized that I am not free. I was the head of the laboratory and later became a lecturer at China Geoscience University. I was at that university for six years, between 1979 and 1985."

Mr. Wu said that after his release from the laogai, "I was quiet, studied hard and never complained about anything. I even received two awards. I never ever spoke of politics.

"Then I was granted the opportunity to go to the University of California at Berkeley as a visiting scholar in the Civil Engineering Department. I remember the day I arrived at the airport in San Francisco. I said, 'God, I am free now!' I got on my knees and kissed the ground. I remember that day. It was Nov. 20, 1985.

"You see, freedom is priceless. I had it, then lost it. Then I finally got it back. You cannot understand what it means to have freedom unless you have lost it. Freedom is quite simple. You can say what you want and go where you want to go."

But Wu's journey to America would test his wits and will. . . .

"When I arrived in America, I only had $40 in my pocket. UC Berkeley officials had said to me to wait one more year and then come over to America, but I could not wait any longer. I had no money, so I had to sleep at the bus station and on a bench in the park. Finally, I found out that I could sleep on the sofa in the library of the university. I could actually take a nap there with the newspaper folded over my face. It was so comfortable."

When UC Berkeley told Wu to wait in China one more year, it was because they wanted to free up money to give him a stipend or help with living arrangements. But Wu was still under surveillance in China and felt the need to leave immediately. He fibbed to UC Berkeley and said, "I have enough money to survive on my own." Of course, Wu did not. Hence, he taught at the university while at the same time living as a homeless person. . . .

While teaching at UC Berkeley, Wu got a job at a donut shop.

"I worked from 9 P.M. till 6 A.M. I used someone else's Social Security number. I had to make 72 dozen donuts per shift, but it was wonderful for me. Finally, I had a roof over my head. I was not homeless anymore. The coffee was free, and the donuts and ice cream, too. I ate so many donuts—for breakfast, lunch and dinner. I can tell you, today, I don't eat donuts anymore!"

Into the Public Eye

"After four months of working, I had saved $1,025. I paid $250 for rent. Then I got a job at a liquor store. I worked from 6 A.M. till 2 P.M. I had half of a night free to sleep in my bed. I told myself, 'If I work hard, I will have a good life because I am now a free man.'"

At that time, Wu "wanted to turn the page and look forward. I didn't want to talk about my experiences in the laogai. There was no congressional testimony, no mass media. But then in 1989 came Tiananmen Square. Americans were shocked, but I was not shocked or surprised.

"I wanted at that time to have a family, a house, a good woman. At my age then, the road ahead of me was less than the road I had passed over. So, I didn't say or do anything politically. Then in 1990, Sen. (Alan) Cranston (D-Calif.) and Sen. (Jesse) Helms (R-N.C.) invited me to testify before the Senate on the laogai."

Thus began Harry Wu's entrance into the public eye as a leading human-rights figure, perhaps the leading figure on earth.

"I went back to China with the '60 Minutes' television program. Ed Bradley came, the first person in the U.S. media to see the slave-labor camps. I said at that time, 'People tirelessly talk about the Nazi Holocaust. In the Soviet gulags, 25 million have been killed, and now that is over. It is common knowledge that all totalitarian regimes—[Soviet dictator Joseph] Stalin, Pol Pot in Cambodia use such camps. Where are the American academics, experts and Sinologists on this issue?' I will tell you exactly where. They identify with Marxism themselves, but moreover, America needs the Chinese market. Free enterprise needs markets.

"By 1992, I was again on the 'Wanted' or 'Black List' in communist China. By 1994, I had a new American passport. I went back to China for five weeks, about 38 days. In 1995, I was charged by the CP with stealing state secrets. They said that I was a 'trouble maker.' But I said to them, 'Why do you say this? I am not speaking about military, economic or governmental information. I am speaking about the slave-labor camps.' At that time, the CP released a government white paper that said, 'We have the best prison system in the world. We help criminals become a newborn person.' So I said to them, 'If you have the best prison system in the world, then I am helping people around the world to understand your prison system.'"

Wu said that at this time, he had accelerated his speaking engagements around the world, explaining the communist totalitarian system and the laogai camps.

Wu's Imprisonment Aided His Cause

Ching-Lee Wu

In the following article published in *Newsweek*, Harry Wu's wife, Ching-Lee Wu, describes how international attention increased when Wu was arrested in China for "stealing state secrets." Wu discusses her husband's arrest and how it drew more support for the campaign against China's forced labor camps that she and her husband have devoted their lives to uncover and abolish.

❧ ❧ ❧

I'm afraid that the leaders of the People's Republic of China don't know the American expression to "shoot yourself in the foot." In any case, that's what they have done by arresting my husband, Harry Wu, and bringing charges of "stealing state secrets" against him. Harry, a survivor of 19 long years in China's Laogai, its system of forced-labor camps, decided to dedicate the rest of his life not just to describing his own experiences in this modern gulag but also to exposing a more frightening reality: how the Laogai, by inflicting unbelievable brutalities on millions of Chinese men and women, still helps cow the rest of the population into submission.

Of late Harry was becoming impatient with himself, afraid he had not made enough progress in his mission, and so at the age of 58 he decided to make one last trip into China to update his information. Three times before, twice in 1991 and once in 1994, he had succeeded in entering China and collecting audiovisual documentation firsthand, even in a camp where he had once been a prisoner himself. This time he failed.

At a border post in northwestern China, police stopped him on June 19, [1999,] with the help of a computer database listing undesirables. They could have turned him back, as they did his assistant. But they didn't; they wanted to punish Harry again for his criticism of the communist system.

Millions of people who had never before heard of Harry Wu now know of him and of the reasons he, a free American citizen, would take such huge risks. The Chinese government used its huge propaganda machine recently to make it seem as if he had "confessed." They titled the 13-minute video "Just See the Lies of Wu Hongda," which was Harry's name as a Chinese citizen.

My heart fell in sadness as I watched an excerpt from that video. In one brief scene that showed him signing an arrest warrant on July 8, Harry appeared normal. In subsequent shots, taken as he was being interrogated by four policemen, Harry was a different man. He was unshaven and looked downcast and weary. He had clearly lost weight. His posture was odd, as though he had been dumped into the chair sideways with his legs tangled beneath him. The voice was his, but strangely low. How many days, or hours each day, had he been interrogated? How much sleep had he been deprived by his interrogators?

On the day this story broke (July 27), reporters in at least 10 separate interviews asked me how I felt about

Harry's "confession." "It's a joke," I said. Chinese propaganda called it a "confession" and the media repeated the false charge, but Harry "confessed" to nothing. In his answers to police, he conceded that a 1994 BBC TV production which he had helped research contained several errors, but denied that he was responsible.

The Laogai Research Foundation, of which Harry is executive director, in January 1995 published an extensive report of his titled "Communist Charity, the Use of Executed Prisoners: Organs in China." That report, which the tape did not mention, cites evidence from other sources, including an internal government document and human-rights organizations, China harvests the organs of executed prisoners for transplants, and supplements that information with testimony that Harry gathered firsthand from Chinese medical personnel and patients.

The communist officials hate Harry because he keeps telling the ugly truth about the communist system in all its horrors. About two months ago, Harry, speaking to a group of business executives in New York City, summarized his indictment of that system this way:

The Laogai serves as the "machinery for crushing human beings physically, psychologically and spiritually." It "is not a prison system; it is a tool for maintaining the Communist Party's totalitarian control." It's an integral part of China's national economy, producing for domestic and foreign markets. Despite a U.S. law prohibiting forced-labor imports and China's signed agreement to respect that law, Laogai products "continue to enter U.S. markets."

These are "lies" that infuriate the communist officials. Harry once warned me that the more his message became known, the more the regime would try to smear him. He told me to prepare for this. Anyone who takes the time to took at the evidence he has accumulated will see that it stands up to scrutiny.

Harry will be surprised to learn how much support his cause has mustered. Both the U.S. Congress and the European Parliament passed strong resolutions urging Harry's immediate release. Australia's foreign minister, Gareth Evans, had his government make very early representations to the Chinese government, both in Beijing and in Melbourne. Archbishop Desmond Tutu intervened personally with the Chinese Trade Mission in South Africa. U.S. Secretary of State Warren Christopher has demanded Harry's release.

In my travels to Washington, Paris and London I pinned yellow ribbons on Newt Gingrich, Dick Gephardt, Margaret Thatcher and other political leaders I had previously seen only on television. On July 29, hundreds of demonstrators marked Free Harry Wu Day in Hong Kong, Sydney, London, Washington, Los Angeles, San Francisco and other cities.

What all this means is that the longer Chinese communists keep Harry, the more interest they will stimulate in the hidden truths about the Laogai. Now, perversely, the Chinese government is helping his cause.

The regime in Beijing wants to silence Harry Wu. It can't, whatever it does. It can't silence other survivors of the Laogai, now coming forward to tell their stories. And it can't silence me.

Natasa Kandic: Fighter Against Human Rights Abuses in Serbia and Kosovo

Kerry Kennedy Cuomo

Natasa Kandic has been vital to exposing human rights abuses in Kosovo and Serbia. Despite extreme danger, she founded and operates the Humanitarian Law Center to gather information about and fight government violations of humanitarian law. Her challenge began in 1992, when ethnic conflict and separatist movements diminished support for a unified Yugoslavian state. Four of six separate republics, which made up Yugoslavia, declared independence and civil wars broke out among Serbs, Croats, and Muslims. Serbian president Slobodan Milosevic called for reunification and began using military power to regain control and force the separate republics back into one territory. According to Kandic, Milosevic used ethnic cleansing, rape, and concentration camps to achieve his purposes. As a lawyer, Kandic has convinced others to testify against Milosevic's soldiers in Serbian court and has consistently spoken out against the repression, bigotry, ethnic cleansing, and other atrocities committed under his regime in the name of war. As she has worked for peace in her country, it has been Kandic's philosophy that human rights are a political issue with serious implications for the future of society. In an interview with Kerry Kennedy Cuomo, Kandic gives an account of the personal battle she has adopted, as she ignores personal fear to give hope to others.

Cuomo is the daughter of the late Robert F. Kennedy, a lawyer, and founder of a human rights foundation.

❦   ❦   ❦

B efore the war years I was involved in political actions in the former Yugoslavia without any knowledge about existing international powers for the protection of human rights. And when the war started in 1991, many of my friends decided to leave the country. I understood their choice, but I felt I had to stay and fight the policies of war itself. I began to travel throughout Yugoslavia, in the beginning to the region of Croatia. I investigated human rights abuses and tried to protect activists, including intellectuals and political parties. When the war later began in Bosnia I focused on minorities and Muslims and their position in Serbia.

In 1992 I decided to formally establish an organization to gather information about the violations of humanitarian law. The idea was to gather evidence, to investigate cases, and to speak out about abuses based on the testimonies we had heard. First we developed a methodology, then established a database. We wanted to be absolutely sure that every allegation was true.

We succeeded in documenting the abuses, but of course we failed to stop the war, or to establish peace. When I documented abuses against the Croats, the regime called me a traitor. When I documented abuses against the Muslims, the regime called me a traitor. When I documented abuses against the Serbs in Croatia, the regime said—nothing. I documented crimes against the Albanians, and of course the regime said that I was a traitor. Lastly, I documented abuses against the Serbs and minorities, much of it against the Roma after the Kosovo war, and the government continued to call me a traitor.

So you see, I don't agree with human rights activists who claim that human rights issues are not political issues. They are crucially important political issues, with serious implications for the future of society. Without respect for human rights and implementation of human rights standards, there won't be democratic changes. Human rights is, in fact, the ultimate political question.

Fear and Isolation

To describe what the last nine years have been in the former Yugoslavia would take days, weeks, months. So let me tell you one or two stories from the recent past. In 1999, I went to an international meeting in Paris and returned on the last flight to Belgrade, just before NATO [the North Atlantic Treaty Organization] started to bomb. Three days into the bombing, I decided to go to Kosovo. The war was on; there were certainly no buses there. So I got in a cab and asked the driver to take me to a town about a hundred kilometers from the border between Serbia and Kosovo, and he agreed. When we finally got there, I asked if he would drive me further, all the way to Pristina. Well, at first he was so afraid. A Serb, he thought the Kosovo Liberation Army was there, that he might be killed. And I then explained to him that only the Serbian police and the Yugoslav army were there. So he decided to do it.

Our first impression of Pristina was really awful. The

only people on the streets were the police and military, only men brandishing weapons, no women at all. I tried to find my office and staff to see what to do. It was so dangerous that we decided to collect everyone and go to Macedonia. But when people heard that I was in Pristina and that I planned to go to Macedonia, there was a big panic. The word spread like a fire and thousands and thousands of cars followed us to the border. Within ten minutes caravans of cars were all around us. But by the time we got to the border it was closed. We told the soldiers that some of us in the cars were Serbs and some Albanians; they were taken aback to see mixed company. But one young soldier warned us to go

A Wall of Denial

For more than ten years Natasa Kandic has risked her life to expose human rights abuses committed by Serbian forces during the breakup of Yugoslavia. Dejan Anastasijevic, a reporter for Time International *in Belgrade, records a few examples.*

Natasa Kandic isn't the most popular woman in Serbia. She's been called a witch and a prostitute, gets more hate mail than junk mail, and recently had to cancel a television appearance due to a bomb threat. "That just goes with the job," says Kandic, 57, who runs the Humanitarian Law Center [HLC] in Belgrade. "I don't think it's me they hate, it's my message."

But she won't shut up. For more than 10 years, Kandic has loudly exposed atrocities and human-rights abuses committed by Serbian forces during the breakup of Yugoslavia. She launched the HLC in 1992, after years as a union activist, and quickly set about producing detailed reports on ethnic cleansing and mass rapes in Bosnia. The day when NATO [the North Atlantic Treaty Organo further, "Because very strange police are here." We were very afraid, and I thought we'd better return immediately to Pristina.

We traveled through empty roads without cars or civilians. Everything was abandoned: the fields, the houses, the villages. Police were hiding because NATO was targeting police forces and military forces. It was very dangerous to travel. But for me it was very important to go out. Based on my experience in Croatia and Bosnia, I know that every effort made in a difficult time will bring some hope. Again, whatever police were there were surprised to see us. Our taxi driver was brilliant. The police checked his identity cards and he began to

nization] started bombing Yugoslavia, in March 1999, was probably the most dangerous moment in her life. "I knew terrible things were about to happen," she remembers. So Kandic jumped into her car and drove some 400 km by herself, dodging NATO missiles and police roadblocks. When she got to Podujevo, in Kosovo, she was shaken by what she saw. "I spoke to women and children who were robbed, then held in burning houses for intimidation. I saw the houses, the rooms in which the bodies had been burned. I saw bones among the ashes."

She believes the truth is slowly trickling out. "The courts are starting to seriously consider some war-crimes cases from Kosovo. And more and more people from security forces are coming out to admit abuses," she says. Lately, Kandic succeeded in persuading several ethnic Albanians, who saw their relatives killed by soldiers, to come and testify against them in a Serbian court. "This will be a benchmark case," she says. "The wall of denial is cracking."

Dejan Anastasijevic, "At War Against War Crimes," *Time International*, April 28, 2003, p. 71.

speak about the situation with the police, always calling them "my brother." The police suspected nothing. This driver was just an ordinary man, without links to human rights organizations or anything. But he courageously just kept driving us through this war zone, never asking why we were there or what we were doing.

He knew I was a Serb and he saw that we were sleeping in Albanian houses shared by Albanians and Serbs. He was confused, but he thought that's okay for Albanians and Serbs to be together. And he wanted to understand, asking my lawyers, "What's happening? What is her job, anyway? Why are you going to Macedonia? What's happened to the Albanians?" And this incredible driver, whom I didn't know before, felt he was safe with me. He said, "I will travel always with you because you are so sure of what you are doing, I don't believe we will ever have trouble."

But I wasn't sure—not really. But I knew it was important to go to Kosovo just to be with the people. I saw their fear and I cannot describe it. They were sitting in their houses without moving. Only a few women had the courage, the strength to go out to buy food. All the men were shut in their apartments, scared of the police, in terror of the paramilitaries, horrified by what might happen to them tomorrow.

I couldn't afford to feel fear because I saw their fear. They kept asking me, "When will you return?" They were completely isolated and I was virtually their only contact with the outside world. I couldn't share my fear because I had an obligation. I spent nights with them, talking about the situation, what to do. I tried hard to convince them to stay, because after war they would need to have a house, to have property, to have their computers, their books. And I think a majority of the people in Pristina who decided to stay did so because of the ten days I was there, talking to people in their houses. It was very important to them that somebody from Belgrade visited, because they knew the danger that effort represented. They knew someone cared, that they were not alone.

After my trip, I returned to Belgrade. I was so surprised to see that people weren't even talking about what was happening in Kosovo. They saw the refugees on CNN, on BBC, but it was unreal to them—nobody even asked me about Kosovo. The level of denial was high.

Every Step Is Important

Then, on March 26, 1999, civil police and military forces had expelled all Albanians from the city of Peje and the refugees fled to Montenegro. So I continued on to Montenegro with my staff to open a temporary office there. I asked my good friends who were Albanian lawyers in Montenegro to work in the office, to begin to interview these expelled Albanians about the expulsions and what happened in Peje, and they accepted.

One stayed to investigate abuses, and two continued on to Albania. And I was happy to see them working in the office, instead of a refugee camp without books, without food, in awful conditions. I left again for Pristina, saying to myself, "Don't think about the police, everything will be all right." I always traveled with the same incredible driver and each time the police stopped us he said, "We are going to Kosovo to pick up some children from our family. How is the situation?" We tried to convince the police that we were Serbians just like them. And they let us go. I was always traveling: Kosovo, Montenegro, Belgrade, and back again, always the same circle.

We talked with people all day and all night, and thousands came to our office, because all of them, as Albanians in Kosovo, were listening to the radio station, Free Europe, which talked about us and the work we were doing. Free Europe was a famous station among Albanians, because they could get objective information from it about events in the former Yugoslavia. When I was in Belgrade, Free Europe always called me about the situation in Kosovo, which was very important, because nobody had any information about what was really happening there. The first time they interviewed me, they prefaced it by asking, "Are you afraid to talk?" I said, "No, I am not afraid. Because I am a fighter. And every step is important."

And you know, after the NATO military intervention, when the troops began to reach the villages, people recognized my voice, not my face, from those broadcasts. Once that saved me in a terrible situation. I was with my Albanian lawyers in a village where sixty people from one family got killed. When all these people came up to us I said "Good afternoon," in Serbo, and people were first shocked, and then very, very angry. It was—menacing. Suddenly, one of them said, "Wait, I recognize your voice. You're the one from the radio." And then all of them came over to me and began to speak of what they had seen and what they suffered.

Profiles · in · History

Human Rights at Work

The UN Commission on Human Rights

Clark M. Eichelberger

The Commission on Human Rights is the part of the United Nations that works to eliminate human rights abuses around the world. The commission promotes and implements the Universal Declaration of Human Rights. Created as a response to the human rights atrocities committed during World War II, this document was adopted by the United Nations and fifty-three nations around the world. In this excerpt from his book, *UN: The First Twenty Years*, Clark M. Eichelberger discusses the history of this document and why it is one of the most internationally accepted documents, in spite of the fact that each nation has a differing view of what basic human rights are, based on its political and economic conditions. Eichelberger further highlights parts of the treaty that are international law and how the Commission on Human Rights works on the difficult task of enforcing human rights around the world.

The operating heart of the United Nations machinery for the promotion of human rights is the Commission on Human Rights. Mrs. Franklin Delano Roosevelt was its first Chairman. It was decided early that the Commission should produce an international bill of human rights. The bill was to be divided into three parts. The first was to be a declaration of human rights, containing fundamental principles to which all peoples could aspire. The second was to be a covenant stating in treaty form those obligations of the declaration that could be so stated, ratified, and become part of international law. The third part of the bill was to contain machinery for enforcement.

The Universal Declaration of Human Rights

The first of the three parts has been achieved. It was near midnight on December 10, 1948, when the General Assembly, meeting in Paris, adopted the Universal Declaration of Human Rights. The delegates had before them the draft, which represented two years of discussion and deliberation in meetings of the Commission. The Declaration was adopted by 48 votes in favor, none against, and 8 abstentions. Before its adoption, Mrs. Roosevelt stated that it was first and foremost a declaration of the basic principles to serve as a common standard for all nations. It might well become the Magna Carta for all mankind.

The wording of the Declaration lacks the moving drama of the American Declaration of Independence or the French Declaration of the Rights of Man, because the United Nations document had to be translatable into five different languages. Granting this handicap, it reads amazingly well.

When the Declaration was adopted, the President of the General Assembly said: "It is the first occasion on which the organized community of nations has made a declaration of human rights and fundamental freedoms, and it has the authority of the body of opinion of the United Nations as a whole, and millions of men, women and children all over the world many miles from Paris and New York will turn for help, guidance and inspiration to this document."

The record will show that his prediction was correct. Indeed, the Declaration marks one of the most remarkable developments in the law of nations. Although not to be considered binding as a treaty, it has developed such authority that it not only is a source of law but is coming to have the force of law. In his Dag Hammarskjöld Memorial Lecture on December 4, 1963, [industrialist] Jacob Blaustein said: "Nevertheless, in the fifteen years since its adoption, it has acquired a political and moral authority which is unequalled by any other international instrument with the exception of the [UN] Charter itself. It is no exaggeration to say that no international instrument has ever received the same acceptance on all levels of society."

Pope John XXIII, referring to the Universal Declaration of Human Rights in his encyclical *Pacem in Terris*, said:

> There is no doubt, however, that the Document represents an important step on the path towards the juridical-political organization of the world Community. For in it, in most solemn form, the dignity of a person is acknowledged to all human beings; and as a consequence there is proclaimed, as a fundamental right, the right of free movement in the search for truth and in the attainment of moral good and of justice, and also the right to a dignified life. . . .

In a memorandum from the Office of Legal Affairs of the United Nations in 1962 it was stated that, while a resolution cannot be made binding upon member states in the sense that a treaty is binding upon them, "However, in view of the greater solemnity and significance of a 'declaration,' it may be considered to impart, on the part of the organ adopting it, a strong expectation that Members of the international community will abide by it. Consequently, in so far as the expectation is gradually justified by State practice, a declaration may by custom become recognized as laying down rules binding upon States."

Various resolutions of the General Assembly have been based upon principles of the Declaration. Many of its articles have been incorporated into peace treaties, trust agreements, and the constitutions of new states. It has been cited as an authority by domestic courts. The member states are expected to use its principles as a standard of measurement in their reports each three years as to the condition of their domestic human rights.

The European Convention for the Protection of Human Rights is based on the Universal Declaration of Human Rights. This document was signed on the fourth of November, 1950, by the foreign ministers of thirteen European states. The Convention represents a significant contribution to the cause of human rights by the Council of Europe. Its Preamble refers to the Declaration of Human Rights "proclaimed by the General Assembly of the United Nations on the tenth of December, 1948. . . ." The Convention then states: "Being resolved, as the Governments of European countries which are likeminded and have a common heritage of political traditions, ideals, freedom and the rule of law, to take the first steps for the collective enforcement of certain of the rights stated in the Universal Declaration. . . ."

The influence of the Declaration goes on. Its principles tend to become part of the common law of nations. . . .

With the adoption of the Declaration statesmen anticipated that work would start on the second part of the international bill of human rights, the Covenant on Human Rights. . . . There early developed a difference of opinion between the older democracies and the new states. The former thought of a covenant on human rights in terms of the basic civil rights which are part of the Western system of justice. The newer states wished to place equal or even greater stress on economic rights. Many of their statesmen spoke from a background of hunger and misery. They insisted that the right to eat and the right of a man to support his family are basic human rights.

While the Western powers were sympathetic to the latter point of view, they doubted that it could be expressed in an international treaty. The economic conditions of many states vary greatly—from poverty to prosperity, from a primitive economy to industrialization. Under such conditions, it is difficult to draft a treaty guaranteeing the right to a job or to social security.

A compromise was reached. It was decided to draft two covenants, one on civil and political rights and one on economic, social, and cultural rights. The two covenants were passed on to the General Assembly . . . for adoption in the year 1954. . . .

Implementation

The third part of the International Bill of Human Rights was to be machinery for enforcement. Implementation is the term generally used to define the clauses looking to some measure of enforcement that would be added to each of the two covenants. In each case a different approach is made to the problem of implementation. As far as the Covenant on Economic, Social, and Cultural Rights is concerned, ratifying nations will be asked only to report to the United Nations on the progress that they make toward the achievement of these rights. Presumably, these reports would be reviewed sympathetically by the Economic and Social Council, with a view to assisting the nations, if necessary, toward achievement of the standards laid down in the Covenant.

However, in the matter of civil and political rights, the measures of implementation may be more forceful and precise. According to the plan as it now exists, there would be established a fact-finding and conciliation organ known as the Human Rights Committee, to which States Parties could complain that other States Parties had violated their obligations under the Covenant. The Human Rights Committee would then attempt to bring about a settlement. Failing this, the Committee would publish a report indicating whether in its opinion there had been a violation of the Covenant. There would also be a right of recourse to the International Court of Justice.

Specific Human Rights Covenants

There have been a number of human rights conventions produced by the United Nations itself or by its Specialized Agencies. It may be worth referring to several of them here.

The Genocide Convention was unanimously adopted by the General Assembly on December 9, 1948. It was then submitted to the members for ratification. The word genocide was coined to describe what the Germans attempted to do—to destroy a whole people on the basis of race, culture, and religion. Over sixty-five governments have deposited instruments of ratification or accession.

In 1950, the General Assembly adopted the Convention on the Political Rights of Women. This Convention was the product of the Commission on the Status of Women. It entitles women to "vote in all elections on equal terms with men, without any discrimination" and "to hold public office and to exercise all public functions, established by national law, on equal terms. . . ."

In 1955, the United Nations, through the Economic and Social Council, proceeded to draft a new anti-slavery convention. It found some so-called "refined" forms of slavery that had not been covered by the original League of Nations antislavery convention. The Convention was adopted in 1956.

Another important convention, "Concerning the Abolition of Forced Labor," was adopted by the International Labor Organization in 1957. This Convention binds ratifying states not to use any form of forced labor "as a means of political coercion or education or as a punishment for holding or expressing political views or views ideologically opposed to the established political, social or economic system; as a method of mobilising and using labour for purposes of economic development; as a means of labour discipline; as a punishment for having participated in strikes; as a means of racial, social, national or religious discrimination.". . .

The Human Rights Score

What is the score on human rights observance throughout the world? The moral insight and determination by which people proclaim a charter of freedom is not maintained in the day-by-day process of carrying the principles of the Declaration into daily life.

Certainly the Charter of the United Nations goes very far in defining human rights and fundamental freedoms as an obligation for the men and nations in the United Nations to advance. Certainly it goes far in setting up machinery for carrying out these obligations. The Declaration of Human Rights probably has had as wide acceptance throughout the world as any document in history outside the Charter of the United Nations itself. Some specific covenants have been drafted and widely ratified. The nations of Western Europe have set up an international system for the enforcement of human rights, including a court.

Large areas of the world remain, however, where the principles of the Declaration may have been adopted but are not understood or carried out. There is still a considerable area of the world where a knock on the door at midnight may mean the concentration camp for fancied political crimes or evil thoughts. There remains a large area where basic civil rights such as freedom from arbitrary arrest or freedom of speech are almost unknown.

Old-fashioned chattel slavery is prevalent in some of the Arab countries of the Middle East. The British Anti-Slavery Society has estimated that seven hundred thousand men and women are held as slaves. So fearful are the nations of offending the Middle East countries, because of their strategic importance, their oil interests, and the Suez Canal, that few voices indeed have been raised to protest this slavery in United Nations meetings. . . .

If the nations advance toward permanent peace, it is inevitable that human rights will be advanced and safeguarded. In an address to the Fiftieth Anniversary Dinner of the American Jewish Committee, [UN secretary-general] Dag Hammarskjöld said, "We know that the question of peace and the question of human rights are closely related. Without recognition of human rights we shall never have peace, and it is only within the framework of peace that human rights can be fully developed."

Amnesty International

Marie Staunton and Sally Fenn

Amnesty International (AI) is an organization of ordinary citizens committed to the advancement of international human rights. In late 1960 a British lawyer named Peter Benenson read a brief newspaper article about two Portuguese students who had been arrested for making a toast to freedom in a Lisbon bar. Benenson decided to start an organization to rescue political prisoners and other victims of government repression around the world; in 1961 Amnesty International was founded. According to Marie Staunton and Sally Fenn, editors of the *Amnesty International Handbook*, AI has become a powerful international lobbying organization for prisoners of conscience and human rights victims. With a network of 1.5 million members in 150 countries around the world, AI puts pressure on governments through letter-writing campaigns, public demonstrations, media outreach, and other methods to promote global human rights. AI's mission is to undertake research and action in preventing physical, mental, or discriminatory human rights abuses. It campaigns for increased accountability of international military, security, and police relations as well as organizes human rights education and awareness programs. In the following excerpt Staunton and Fenn review the history of AI and its main objectives.

Marie Staunton and Sally Fenn, *Amnesty International Handbook*. Claremont, CA: Hunter House, 1991. Copyright © 1991 by Amnesty International. All rights reserved. Reproduced by permission.

🐝 🐝 🐝

Wen Amnesty International was founded in 1961 it was called "one of the larger lunacies of our time." It seemed absurd that ordinary people could help men, women, and children they had never seen in countries they had never visited by writing polite letters to foreign governments. But it works: Since its inception, Amnesty International has adopted or investigated more than 42,000 prisoner cases and we have been able to close more than 38,000. Today, human rights are firmly established on the international agenda. No longer can governments turn a blind eye when their human rights records are called into question.

More than one million people worldwide, from school children to pensioners of all races and politics, in 150 countries, are now working for Amnesty International's three goals:

— The release of prisoners of conscience. These are people detained for their beliefs, color, sex, ethnic origin, language, or religion who have not used or advocated violence

— Fair and prompt trials for all political prisoners

— An end to the death penalty and torture or other cruel, inhuman, and degrading treatment or punishment of all prisoners without reservation.

These goals are the essence of Amnesty International's mandate and your help is needed to achieve them. As with any struggle, what determines whether the human rights movement advances or retreats is, in the end, the balance of forces. Our forces do not consist of armies or governments, but of men and women who are prepared to commit themselves to the struggle for human rights. When a victim is released from unjust imprisonment or is granted a fair trial, human rights score victories. When torture ceases or executions are prohibited, human rights take a great step forward.

"I feel like a different person, just knowing there is a group that intervenes for human rights," wrote the wife of a political prisoner held in Eastern Europe. "A letter such as one from Amnesty International gives a person strength and makes one feel human again." The prisoner, arrested for criticizing his government in 1981, was freed in April 1987. For six years, two Amnesty International local volunteer groups, one in the Netherlands and one in Canada, had worked for his release. "Mainly I owe my early release to you and your work on my case," he wrote recently to members of the groups.

The Founding of Amnesty International

In November 1960, Peter Benenson, a 40-year-old British lawyer, read a newspaper report about two Portuguese students in Lisbon during the Salazar dictatorship. They had been arrested and sentenced to seven years' imprisonment for raising their glasses in public in a toast to freedom.

Incensed by this, Benenson began to consider ways in which the Portuguese authorities—and other oppressive regimes—could be persuaded to release such victims of injustice. His idea was to bombard governments with letters of protest at the imprisonment of prisoners of conscience.

Together with Eric Baker, a prominent English Quaker, Louis Blom-Cooper, a renowned lawyer, and others, he launched a one-year campaign called "Appeal for Amnesty, 1961" to highlight the fate of political prisoners worldwide.

The campaign was launched with an article which appeared in the *London Observer* on May 28, 1961, focusing on eight "forgotten prisoners." The article received a tremendous response: letters of support and money arrived, details of many, many more prisoners were sent, and volunteers eager to work for the release of prisoners of conscience came forward. Amnesty International was born.

Amnesty International is a worldwide campaign for victims of human rights abuse. Its volunteer groups adopt prisoners of conscience, work to end torture and the death penalty throughout the world, and put pressure on governments through letter writing, public demonstration, media outreach, and other techniques.

Amnesty has more than 4,200 local groups around the world. At the end of November 1990, Amnesty International was working on more than 3,000 cases involving more than 4,500 individuals in 83 countries. The good news was that 1,296 cases were closed in the first eleven months of 1990.

Increasingly, Amnesty groups in trade unions, on college and high school campuses, in churches, and among doctors, lawyers, teachers, women, and those working with children, are coordinating their efforts. Using their contacts and their ingenuity, they bring pressure to bear on governments to respect human rights. An increasing number of groups of police officers or ex-military personnel use their experience and persuasive powers to stop their counterparts in other countries abusing human rights.

In this work, Amnesty's mandate to remain independent, impartial, and voluntary is carefully safeguarded, and all members of Amnesty International obey clear rules when working for individuals.

Central to this is financial independence—no money is now accepted from governments. The whole international organization, which employs 250 researchers and has offices in 46 countries, is run entirely on contributions from its members and supporters and hundreds of thousands of donations from around the world. And all the fundraising is the responsibility of the movement's groups and sections—there is no central fundraising program. Each national section solicits its own members, produces and sells its own keyrings and T-shirts, promotes concerts, runs television campaigns, and does whatever else it can to raise money for victims of human rights abuse.

To ensure impartiality, no AI member works on behalf of prisoners held in their own country. However, they can address their own countries' human rights policies. In 1989, for example, during a worldwide campaign to abolish the death penalty, many sections lobbied their own governments to repeal the death penalty. National sections also urged their governments to sign and ratify human rights treaties.

It is essential that Amnesty groups show that they are politically and geographically balanced by campaigning to end patterns of abuse in a range of countries across the geo-political spectrum.

How Amnesty Works

The work of Amnesty International is carried out by an army of volunteers, making AI a truly voluntary organization. The first step in any Amnesty campaign is obtaining reliable information. This is done by scanning official sources, sending missions to a country, sending lawyers to observe trials, and by interviewing witnesses. Once the information has been checked and verified, it is released to the public. As word spreads about the human rights violations involved, the pressure on the government builds. Sometimes government authorities respond to AI concerns in private meetings with representatives of Amnesty International; sometimes they respond directly to the volunteers who send them letters.

For example, members of local groups in Hong Kong

and Mexico who participated in the campaign against human rights violations in Iran received acknowledgment of their letters from the office of the Iranian Speaker of Parliament. An Iranian provincial public relations official also corresponded with group members in Denmark and the Federal Republic of Germany.

Many state governors and other officials in the United States responded to Amnesty's campaign to end the death penalty here. The Norwegian Section arranged television broadcasts of interviews with governors of states which permit the death penalty. In Mauritius, the campaign received prime-time television coverage. Editorials and news articles published throughout the United States helped to focus debate on the death penalty as a violation of a basic human right.

Human rights activists worldwide use their own creativity to serve human rights campaigns. In Bangladesh, members sponsored a poster exhibition to draw public attention to an adopted prisoner of conscience. In Luxembourg, members invited the public to buy Amnesty International candles and place them in windows to commemorate Human Rights Day, December 10. Thousands of Spanish schools participated in a human rights essay contest organized by Amnesty, and Japanese members held a walkathon for prisoners of conscience worldwide.

The human rights championed by Amnesty International are the same that most governments have already promised to uphold. In 1948, the nations of the world united to proclaim the Universal Declaration of Human Rights in response to the horrifying events of World War II. This Declaration begins: "Everyone shall live free and equal in dignity and rights." In signing the Declaration, the nations of the world also undertook to help obtain the range of human rights, from freedom of conscience to a free wage, not just for their own citizens but also for those in other countries.

But human rights are too important—and vulnerable—to be left to governments. Governments will always find excuses to ignore human rights. It is ordinary people, not only in international organizations like Amnesty but also in the many national human rights organizations throughout the world, who must ensure that the Universal Declaration of Human Rights is upheld. . . .

Human Rights Changes Around the Globe

1990 was a watershed year for human rights. The news that emerged from Eastern Europe, South America, and South Africa all fed a new optimism. The Berlin Wall had just fallen. In Chile, Augusto Pinochet, defeated in a national plebiscite, was forced to turn over the reins of power to a civilian government. And a former Amnesty International prisoner of conscience, Vaclav Havel, became Czechoslovakia's first democratic President since the late 1940s.

Half a world away, in South Africa, Nelson Mandela—perhaps the world's most famous political prisoner—was released, and a meaningful political dialogue began on the future of that country.

But there was a downside. The vast political changes sweeping Europe unleashed nationalist tensions that had long been repressed. No one could say for certain how the new nationalist fervor would affect human rights in the region. There were violent clashes throughout Eastern Europe. In Yugoslavia, disturbances in Kosovo Province during January and February left 30 dead. Some of the republics within the Soviet Union began to call for independence. Soviet attempts to crack down on these secessionist movements sometimes led to violence, while in other parts of the country long-hostile ethnic communities turned to force to settle their ancient animosities.

In Southeast Asia, there were extensive reports of torture in Myanmar (Burma), where a military government continued in power despite losing a national election. In the 18 months preceding the elections, the authorities arrested and detained thousands of supporters of nonviolent political parties. China began to put on trial many long-term dissidents, some of whom had taken part in pro-democracy demonstrations the previous spring.

Meanwhile, in Central America, El Salvador's death squads continued their murderous activity in 1990, despite pledges by the government that steps were being taken to prevent and investigate human rights abuses.

One event overshadowed all others. On August 2, Iraq invaded Kuwait. The invasion and subsequent occupation of Kuwait resulted in a wave of serious human rights violations, and the world was witness to a military confrontation in the Persian Gulf. As war clouds gathered throughout the autumn there was growing concern for human rights, both in the Middle East and beyond.

The old year ended on a somber note. War broke out early in the new year. The wave of optimism that had brought in 1990 had dissolved into a more sober reality in 1991.

As Amnesty International gets ready to mark its 30th Anniversary, there will be no letting up in the volume or intensity of the work to be done.

Jimmy Carter

Millard Grimes

In this article excerpted from *Georgia Trend*, writer Millard Grimes examines Jimmy Carter's political career as a senator, a governor, and the thirty-ninth president of the United States. Grimes contends that although Carter's presidency was plagued by a worldwide energy crisis, rising cost of living, and Cold War tensions, Carter is an outstanding former president. Carter's postpresidential career has been focused on promoting peace and human rights through the Carter Center in Atlanta, which he founded with his wife, Rosalynn. The center works to promote peace, constitutional democracy, and human rights around the world.

❦ ❦ ❦

James Earl (Jimmy) Carter is the only Georgian to serve as president of the United States. He was elected to a four-year term in November 1976, narrowly defeating President Gerald Ford, the incumbent Republican, who succeeded to the presidency in 1974 after the resignation of President Richard Nixon.

Carter, who had served one term as governor of Georgia (1971–75), was regarded as the darkest of dark

Millard Grimes, "The 39th President: Jimmy Carter 1924-Present," *Georgia Trend*, January 2000, p. 20. Copyright © 2000 by *Georgia Trend*. Reproduced by permission.

horses when he announced for president, but in a primary campaign mapped out and implemented by Georgians Hamilton Jordan and Jody Powell, Carter came in first among several better-known candidates in the Iowa caucuses and the New Hampshire primary, thus emerging as the clear front-runner and eventual nominee.

Carter was defeated in a bid for re-election in 1980 by Republican Ronald Reagan. Leaving the presidency at the fairly young age of 56, Carter has become one of the most successful and valuable former presidents, and is widely recognized as the "outstanding" former president in U.S. history.

He established The Carter Center and Library in Atlanta, and The Center has become a major force for the promotion of peace and human rights in the world. The Center and Library also are among the most popular tourist attractions in Atlanta.

Carter has become a prolific author in his post–White House years, writing and publishing 12 books, ranging from accounts of his political career and presidency, to books on fly-fishing and aging, plus a book of poems. His wife, Rosalynn, a successful author in her own right, co-wrote two books with him, and is the co-founder and chair of The Carter Center.

A 1946 graduate of the U.S. Naval Academy, Carter returned to his home town of Plains to take over the family farming interests when his father died in 1953. He entered politics as a member of the Sumter County school board, and was elected to the state Senate in 1962, after successfully contesting the original vote count as being fraudulent. He first ran for governor in 1966, finishing third in the Democratic primary behind former Gov. Ellis Arnall and Lester Maddox, the eventual winner. In 1970, he defeated former Gov. Carl Sanders for the Democratic nomination and then defeated Hal Suit, the Republican candidate, in the general election.

As governor, Carter pushed through a major reorganization of state government, and became an instant national figure by declaring in his inauguration speech "that the time for racial discrimination is over."

Carter's Presidency

Carter's four years as president were more successful than is generally accepted 20 years later. The achievements were notable, but the challenges and failures were daunting and more memorable. Carter came to the presidency when a world energy crisis was already underway, and it was soon magnified by the revolution in Iran, which cut off that country's oil supplies for a time, doubling the price of fuel in the U.S. Carter made energy conservation a centerpiece of his domestic policy, which was not popular and also hampered recovery from the economic recession of the mid-1970s.

At the same time, Carter courageously and strongly supported human rights abroad; the unpopular Panama Canal treaty, which would eventually turn over the canal to Panama; recognition of the Communist regime as the legitimate government of China; and peace talks between Israel and Egypt.

His outstanding achievement was the Camp David Peace Accords, which he personally hammered out in a series of meetings with Israeli Prime Minister Menachem Begin and Egyptian President Anwar Sadat, both of whom won the Nobel Peace Prize that year— but not Carter, who was the essential player in the process. The accords had their critics at the time and did not help Carter in his 1980 re-election bid, but in the 20 years since they were signed, there has not been a major conflict between Israel and its Arab neighbors, while in the previous 20 years there were four major wars (in 1948, 1956, 1967 and 1973).

Most of all, Carter was victimized by the rising cost

of living, caused in large measure by the higher oil prices. He named Paul Volcker to chair the Federal Reserve Board and told him to tame inflation. Volcker's solution was to raise interest rates and squeeze the money supply, which resulted initially in even higher inflation and interest rates that finally peaked at 21% in

---

Peace Laureate

Kenneth T. Walsh, a writer for U.S. News & World Report, *reviews Jimmy Carter's "untiring" social activism that led to his being awarded the Nobel Peace Prize in 2002. Walsh highlights Carter's work.*

Since leaving the White House, Carter has devoted himself to writing books and building Atlanta's Carter Center, a think tank that combines scholarly studies with social activism in more than 60 nations. The center specializes in helping people in poverty, people who suffer from diseases that other institutions ignore, such as river blindness and Guinea worm, and people who are often abused or neglected by their rulers.

In a . . . *U.S. News* interview, Carter described his post-presidential years as satisfying but expressed special pride in his one presidential term. He noted that he had kept the peace under difficult circumstances, never ordering the dropping of a bomb or the launching of a missile. As for the humiliation of having 52 Americans held hostage in Iran for 444 days and the failed mission to rescue them—all of which contributed to his 1980 loss—he said he was gratified that all the captives were eventually released unharmed.

Kenneth T. Walsh, "Peace Laureate," *U.S. News & World Report*, October 21, 2002, p. 59.

Reagan's first years as president.

Carter had prescribed the necessary but bitter medicine, and he also began deregulation of gasoline prices in the U.S., eventually leading to lower prices at the tank, but Reagan got the credit. Carter also arranged the release of U.S. hostages in Iran, without the loss of a single hostage's life, but the release came after his defeat in the November election.

Postpresidential Career

Carter is certainly more highly regarded for his postpresidential work and, indeed, he has become one of the most beloved and respected Americans throughout the world, due to his personal efforts and the work of The Carter Center on behalf of human rights and constitutional democracy. He and Rosalynn have led many teams that monitored elections in nations where voting is not only rare but often hazardous.

In [1999], The Carter Center has begun implementing a landmark agreement with the Chinese government to standardize its 9,300,000 village elections.

Carter, especially in [the 1990s], has gained an unchallenged position as the preeminent peacemaker of his generation, long since making a Nobel Prize irrelevant in validating his achievements, but providing a standard by which the Nobel's annual recipients can be measured—and usually found lacking.

Despite his standing in the global community, Carter has still not found broad popularity among his fellow Georgians, as demonstrated by the struggles of his ambitious Atlanta Project, designed to improve . . . conditions in the inner city. He is not hesitant to criticize U.S. policies he believes are wrong, and in [an] . . . interview with the Atlanta media, he called the U.S. "the stingiest nation" on foreign aid to needy countries.

"Foreign aid has become an epithet in this country,

and no public figure can even support foreign aid except to a few countries. Norway, for instance, spends nine times as much on foreign aid as the U.S., which is the richest nation in the world," Carter said.

"The most serious problem for the new millennium is the growing gap between the rich and poor nations, but it can hardly be brought up in political discussions, much less seriously addressed.". . .

The former president is certainly an example of the virtues of staying active in later years. He remains an influential force in Georgia as The Carter Center brings many world leaders to conferences each year, and most importantly his name is a byword in remote nations of the world—such as in Africa, where The Center has a project to eradicate Guinea worm—in which hope has always been rare and fleeting, and the attention of a former U.S. president is in itself a sign that hope has not vanished.

The Carter Center

Faith McLellan

The Carter Center was originally founded in partnership with former U.S. president Jimmy Carter, his wife Rosalynn, and Emory University in Atlanta, Georgia, to work for peace, democracy, health, and human rights. Carter told Faith McLellan, author of the following article, that it soon became evident that peace, freedom, human rights, and human suffering could not be treated as separate issues.

McLellan reviews some of the international health and human rights issues that compose the work of the Carter Center and discusses Carter's goals for the center. McLellan writes for the *Lancet*, a biomedical publication.

🐦 🐦 🐦

Jimmy Carter, winner of the 2002 Nobel Peace Prize, and 39th President of the USA [was] so little known when he ran for the office that historian Douglas Brinkley observed, "it was like picking a name out of the phone book". Now, of course, his name is known around the world. By contrast with most of his peers, though, it isn't simply because of the political office he held. Indeed, Carter's post-presidency has garnered perhaps as much attention as his elected role. After

Faith McLellan, "Jimmy Carter and Life After the US Presidency," *Lancet*, vol. 361, March 29, 2003, p. 1,108. Copyright © 2003 by The Lancet Ltd. Reproduced by permission.

Ronald Reagan trounced his bid for a second presidential term, Carter and his wife, Rosalynn, returned to Georgia, where they founded, in partnership with Emory University, The Carter Center. This Atlanta-based non-profit organisation celebrated its 20th anniversary [in 2002]. It works for peace, democracy, and health and human rights in 65 countries around the world, 35 of which are in Africa.

The Center now has a staff of 150 and a yearly budget of $35 million. It works in partnership with or receives donations from various public and private organisations and individuals.

Carter told *The Lancet* that he first intended the Center to concentrate solely on peace issues, but it soon became evident, in the developing world especially, that there was "no way to separate the major elements of life—peace, freedom, human rights, and alleviation of human suffering". Thus, the health programmes, which how comprise more than half the Center's budget, were born.

The Carter Process

Carter's status as a former president has given him, he observes, "unanticipated simultaneous access both to the poorest people and to top leaders". He approaches heads of state directly about proposed health programmes, all of which he has personally approved, and asks them to recruit their entire cabinet to assist in the effort. Aversion to the politics of a country, or pressure to avoid a specific area, is no deterrent. Carter says he goes wherever he sees a need, ignoring political considerations and other obstacles that might stand in the way.

After the involved parties have agreed to proceed with a new project, the Center sends one foreigner into the country, who acts as the resident technical adviser and trains local people to do the work. It collaborates with national ministries of health and regional and local affiliates to provide staff and infrastructure.

At present there are nine health programmes, some of which are highlighted below: dracunculiasis (guinea worm); onchocerciasis (river blindness); trachoma; lymphatic filariasis (elephantiasis); schistosomiasis (snail fever); public health training in Ethiopia; an international task force on disease eradication; an agriculture programme; and a mental health programme, which Rosalynn Carter heads up.

The guinea worm programme is the oldest and most successful of the health projects. It is also acknowledged as a favourite by many, mainly, as Donald Hopkins, Associate Executive Director of the health programmes, points out, because of the way it has brought about behavioural change. The programme serves as a model of ways to approach people, especially those liv-

Jimmy Carter shakes hands with President Sadat of Egypt (left) and Prime Minister Begin of Israel (right) in 1979 upon the signing of a peace treaty between their two countries.

ing in rural communities, to get them to change the behaviours that allow disease to flourish. "People are rational, and if approached in a reasonable way, will change their lives for the better", Hopkins said. The guinea worm workers are also regarded as an unusually passionate bunch. They wear clothing emblazoned with guinea worm designs or T-shirts with anti-guinea worm messages in multiple languages. And they were once greeted in an African village by a little girl bearing a sign that read, "Watch out, guinea worm—Jimmy Carter's around!" When the project began, in 1986, there were about 3.5 million cases of this parasitic, water-borne disease in Africa and Asia. Carter recalled a village he visited in Ghana, where 300 of the 500 residents had the disease; the first person he saw, memorably, was a young woman with a guinea worm emerging from her nipple. One year later, there were no cases in that village. Now, thanks to education about contaminated drinking water, the use of cloth or pipe filters, and, in Sudan, a 4-month-long Carter-negotiated "Guinea Worm Cease-Fire", the worldwide incidence has been reduced by 98%, with fewer than 75 000 cases remaining. Guinea worm is now expected to be the first parasitic disease to be completely eradicated.

New Emphasis

As the guinea worm programme winds down, river blindness, a parasitic disease spread by blackflies in fast-flowing river waters and endemic to some African countries, the Arabian peninsula, and the Americas, will become the Center's major health emphasis. The source of the disease can be eliminated by some insecticides, and a single yearly dose (or, in the Americas, twice yearly) of ivermectin (donated by [the pharmaceutical company] Merck) prevents its development. 2007 is the target date for eradication in Latin America.

Rosalynn Carter, who has worked on mental health issues for longer than 25 years including during her tenure as First Lady, provides the leadership for the Center's mental health programmes, which she describes as now moving "from advocacy to action". The programmes, which forge partnerships among clinical, policy, and public arenas, have three main goals: to eliminate stigma; to achieve complete insurance coverage parity; and to institute early screening for mental and behavioural disorders. Other goals, according to Thomas Bornemann, director of the mental health programmes, include strengthening the organisation and financing of mental health services; incorporating evidence into practice; and developing ways to get greater funding for a research agenda.

All the health programmes are evaluated yearly. The national coordinators come together to update each other on their latest surveillance, prevalence, and monitoring data, and to describe the training, education, treatment, and evaluation activities undertaken in the previous year. Programmes are then modified accordingly.

Ongoing surveillance is a hallmark of the Center's work, with evaluation at present focused mainly on "process measures rather than outcome measures", according to health policy researcher Kevin Frick, of the Johns Hopkins Bloomberg School of Public Health. Outcome measures are more difficult, and it takes time to show sustained changes in behavioural and environmental factors. Frick looks forward to seeing future data on economic analysis, with fundamental data especially about the flow of resources through local governments; this kind of information would be particularly useful for others who wish to replicate the Center's programmes. . . .

The personalities of the Carters and their heavy involvement in the details of the Center's work are major factors in its success. But with both of them in their late 70s, and their roles diminishing, questions about the future of the Center are taking on a newly urgent dimension. Carter said he hopes the Center will retain a narrow focus on the most important issues that are being ignored by others; remain flexible and undeterred by political proprieties; continue to insist on tight connections between countries' top leaders and workers at the village level; and ultimately bring "peace, health, and hope to the most disadvantaged". Accomplishing these lofty goals will require a well groomed and well connected successor, who will need what [medical missionary William] Foege has described as the three vital ingredients for its success: "activism, the ability to get academic input, and access". Foege says the Carters' successor will probably have to correct for a deficit in the access area, since former presidents enjoy an obvious advantage in that area. Moreover, that person will also have to fill not just one, but two, pairs of enormous shoes—belonging to a peripatetic couple of prodigious energy, profound organisational skill, and a manner that is characteristically gracious but obviously backed by an iron will. It's going to be a hard act to follow. But the need for "waging peace, fighting disease, and building hope"—the Center's motto—shows no sign whatever of abating.

Appendix of Documents

Document 1: My Faith in Nonviolence

In the following speech Mohandas Gandhi discusses his faith in nonviolence.

Non-violence is a weapon of the strong. With the weak it might easily be hypocrisy. Fear and love are contradictory terms. Love is reckless in giving away, oblivious as to what it gets in return. Love wrestles with the world as with the self and ultimately gains a mastery over all other feelings. My daily experience, as of those who are working with me, is that every problem lends itself to solution if we are determined to make the law of truth and non-violence the law of life. For truth and non-violence are, to me, faces of the same coin.

M.K. Gandhi, *Non-Violent Resistance.* New York: Schocken Books, 1961, p. 384.

Document 2: I Have a Dream

It was the one-hundredth anniversary of the Emancipation Proclamation, yet racial unrest put America on the brink of civil war again. Racial hatred and intolerance of black citizens caused Martin Luther King Jr. to call America a sick society. Before the Lincoln Memorial in Washington, D.C., on August 28, 1963, King delivered his "I Have a Dream" speech as the keynote address to the March on Washington. It is excerpted here.

Fivescore years ago, a great American, in whose symbolic shadow we stand today, signed the Emancipation Proclamation. This momentous decree came as a great beacon light of hope to millions of Negro slaves who had been seared in the flames of withering injustice. It came as a joyous daybreak to end the long night of their captivity.

But one hundred years later, the Negro still is not free; one hundred years later, the life of the Negro is still sadly crippled by the manacles of segregation and the chains of discrimination; one hundred years later, the Negro lives on a lonely island of poverty in the midst of a vast ocean of material prosperity; one hundred years later, the Negro is still languished in the corners of American society and finds himself in exile in his own land. . . .

We can never be satisfied as long as our bodies, heavy with fatigue of travel, cannot gain lodging in the motels of the highways and the hotels of the cities. We cannot be satisfied as long as the Negro's basic mobility is from a smaller ghetto to a larger one.

We can never be satisfied as long as our children are stripped of their selfhood and robbed of their dignity by signs stating "for whites only." We cannot be satisfied as long as a Negro in Mississippi cannot vote and a Negro in New York believes he has nothing for which to vote. No, we are not satisfied, and we will not be satisfied until justice rolls down like waters and righteousness like a mighty stream.

Martin Luther King Jr., *I Have a Dream: Writings and Speeches That Changed the World*, edited by James Melvin Washington. San Francisco: HarperCollins, 1992, pp. 102, 104.

Document 3: War as a Human Rights Crime

As president of Ireland and later as chairperson for the UN Commission on Human Rights, Mary Robinson addressed what she considered an appropriate response to strengthening human rights around the world.

In many parts of the world, the major problems to be tackled as part of the humanitarian agenda include poverty and famine, pollution and environmental pressures, ethnic conflict, excessive military expenditures, inadequate water supply, AIDS, drugs, refugees, and massive migration.

To confront them effectively, governments, NGOs [nongovernmental organizations], international organizations, and especially the United Nations, must work closely together with a greater degree of commitment, cohesion, and cooperation. . . .

What is needed, therefore, is a people-to-people approach, supplementing and influencing governmental and institutional responses. Ordinary people in many countries—including here in the United States—have responded generously to the images of starving people by donating money to the various aid agencies. This is one important people-to-people response—but it is not enough. A striking feature of our modern world is the potential level of communication and interaction which could be harnessed to resolve problems. . . . Western rural communities have practical experiences which are of relevance to rural communities in developing countries. Inner city groups build up an expertise which can be helpful to local communities in the cities and slums of developing countries. We have the potential to create informal, flexible networks of support as channels of communication, practical aid, and technical assistance.

The true price of the access and immediacy of television and newspaper images showing what is happening around the world is to place on each of us responsibility for our response to those images. There are very few of us who cannot do something, however modest, as an assumption of individual responsibility and of engagement. If whole populations became engaged through modest individual responses, political priorities would inevitably be affected, and necessary political will for collective action engendered.

Mary Robinson, "The Appropriate Response to Humanity," *Presidents & Prime Ministers*, July/August 1993, p. 15.

Document 4: The Universal Declaration of Human Rights

The Universal Declaration of Human Rights set an international standard for human rights. This document was originally ratified by fifty-three countries eager to make a statement on human rights following the atrocities of World War II.

Preamble

Whereas recognition of the inherent dignity and of the equal and inalienable rights of all members of the human family is the foundation of freedom, justice and peace in the world,

Whereas disregard and contempt for human rights have resulted in barbarous acts which have outraged the conscience of mankind, and the advent of a world in which human beings shall enjoy freedom of speech and belief and freedom from fear and want has been proclaimed as the highest aspiration of the common people,

Whereas it is essential, if man is not to be compelled to have recourse, as a last resort, to rebellion against tyranny and oppression, that human rights should be protected by the rule of law,

Whereas it is essential to promote the development of friendly relations between nations,

Whereas the peoples of the United Nations have in the Charter reaffirmed their faith in fundamental human rights, in the dignity and worth of the human person and in the equal rights of men and women and have determined to promote social progress and better standards of life in larger freedoms,

Whereas member States have pledged themselves to achieve, in co-operation with the United Nations, the promotion of universal respect for and observance of human rights and fundamental freedoms,

Whereas a common understanding of these rights and freedoms is of the greatest importance for the full realization of this pledge,

Now therefore,

The General Assembly

Proclaims this Universal Declaration of Human Rights as a common standard of achievement for all peoples and all nations, to the end that every individual and every organ of society, keeping this Declaration constantly in mind, shall strive by teaching and education to promote respect for these rights and freedoms and by progressive measures, national and international, to secure their universal and effective recognition and observance, both among the peoples of member States themselves and among the peoples of territories under their jurisdiction.

Article 1
All human beings are born free and equal in dignity and rights. They are endowed with reason and conscience and should act towards one another in a spirit of brotherhood.

Article 2
1. Everyone is entitled to all the rights and freedoms set forth in this Declaration, without distinction of any kind, such as race, colour, sex, language, religion, political or other opinion, national or social origin, property, birth or other status.

2. Furthermore, no distinction shall be made on the basis of the political, jurisdictional or international status of the country or territory to which a person belongs, whether it be independent, trust, non-self-governing or under any other limitation of sovereignty.

Article 3
Everyone has the right to life, liberty and security of person.

Article 4
No one shall be held in slavery or servitude; slavery and the slave trade shall be prohibited in all their forms.

Article 5
No one shall be subjected to torture or to cruel, inhuman or degrading treatment or punishment.

Article 6
Everyone has the right to recognition everywhere as a person before the law.

Article 7
All are equal before the law and are entitled without any discrimination to equal protection of the law. All are entitled to equal protection against any discrimination in violation of

this Declaration and against any incitement to such discrimination.

Article 8
Everyone has the right to an effective remedy by the competent national tribunals for acts violating the fundamental rights granted him by the constitution or by law.

Article 9
No one shall be subjected to arbitrary arrest, detention or exile.

Article 10
Everyone is entitled in full equality to a fair and public hearing by an independent and impartial tribunal, in the determination of his rights and obligations and of any criminal charge against him.

Article 11
1. Everyone charged with a penal offence has the right to be presumed innocent until proved guilty according to law in a public trial at which he has had all the guarantees necessary for his defence.

   2. No one shall be held guilty of any penal offence on account of any act or omission which did not constitute a penal offence, under national or international law, at the time when it was committed. Nor shall a heavier penalty be imposed than the one that was applicable at the time the penal offence was committed.

Article 12
No one shall be subjected to arbitrary interference with his privacy, family, home or correspondence, nor to attacks upon his honour and reputation. Everyone has the right to the protection of the law against such interference or attacks.

Article 13
1. Everyone has the right to freedom of movement and residence within the borders of each State.

2. Everyone has the right to leave any country, including his own, and to return to his country.

Article 14

1. Everyone has the right to seek and to enjoy in other countries asylum from persecution.

2. This right may not be invoked in the case of prosecutions genuinely arising from non-political crimes or from acts contrary to the purposes and principles of the United Nations.

Article 15

1. Everyone has the right to a nationality.

2. No one shall be arbitrarily deprived of his nationality nor denied the right to change his nationality.

Article 16

1. Men and women of full age, without any limitation due to race, nationality or religion, have the right to marry and to found a family. They are entitled to equal rights as to marriage, during marriage and at its dissolution.

2. Marriage shall be entered into only with free and full consent of the intending spouses.

3. The family is the natural and fundamental group unit of society and is entitled to protection by society and the State.

Article 17

1. Everyone has the right to own property alone as well as in association with others.

2. No one shall be arbitrarily deprived of his property.

Article 18

Everyone has the right to freedom of thought, conscience and religion; this right includes freedom to change his religion or belief, and freedom, either alone or in community with others and in public or private, to manifest his religion or belief in teaching, practice, worship and observance.

Article 19
Everyone has the right to freedom of opinion and expression; this right includes freedom to hold opinions without interference and to seek, receive and impart information and ideas through any media and regardless of frontiers.

Article 20
1. Everyone has the right to freedom of peaceful assembly and association.

2. No one may be compelled to belong to an association.

Article 21
1. Everyone has the right to take part in the government of his country, directly or through freely chosen representatives.

2. Everyone has the right to equal access to public service in his country.

3. The will of the people shall be the basis of the authority of government; this will shall be expressed in periodic and genuine elections which shall be by universal and equal suffrage and shall be held by secret vote or by equivalent free voting procedures.

Article 22
Everyone, as a member of society, has the right to social security and is entitled to realization, through national effort and international co-operation and in accordance with the organization and resources of each State, of the economic, social and cultural rights indispensable for his dignity and the free development of his personality.

Article 23
1. Everyone has the right to work, to free choice of employment, to just and favourable conditions of work and to protection against unemployment.

2. Everyone, without any discrimination, has the right to equal pay for equal work.

3. Everyone who works has the right to just and favourable remuneration ensuring for himself and his family an existence worthy of human dignity, and supplemented, if

necessary, by other means of social protection.

4. Everyone has the right to form and to join trade unions for the protection of his interests.

Article 24
Everyone has the right to rest and leisure, including reasonable limitation of working hours and periodic holidays with pay.

Article 25
1. Everyone has the right to a standard of living adequate for the health and well-being of himself and of his family, including food, clothing, housing and medical care and necessary social services, and the right to security in the event of unemployment, sickness, disability, widowhood, old age or other lack of livelihood in circumstances beyond his control.

2. Motherhood and childhood are entitled to special care and assistance. All children, whether born in or out of wedlock, shall enjoy the same social protection.

Article 26
1. Everyone has the right to education. Education shall be free, at least in the elementary and fundamental stages. Elementary education shall be compulsory. Technical and professional education shall be made generally available and higher education shall be equally accessible to all on the basis of merit.

2. Education shall be directed to the full development of the human personality and to the strengthening of respect for human rights and fundamental freedoms. It shall promote understanding, tolerance and friendship among all nations, racial or religious groups, and shall further the activities of the United Nations for the maintenance of peace.

3. Parents have a prior right to choose the kind of education that shall be given to their children.

Article 27
1. Everyone has the right freely to participate in the cultural life of the community, to enjoy the arts and to share in scientific advancement and its benefits.

2. Everyone has the right to the protection of the moral and material interests resulting from any scientific, literary or artistic production of which he is the author.

Article 28
Everyone is entitled to a social and international order in which the rights and freedoms set forth in this Declaration can be fully realized.

Article 29
1. Everyone has duties to the community in which alone the free and full development of his personality is possible.

2. In the exercise of his rights and freedoms, everyone shall be subject only to such limitations as are determined by law sorely for the purpose of securing due recognition and respect for the rights and freedoms of others and of meeting the just requirements of morality, public order and the general welfare in a democratic society.

3. These rights and freedoms may in no case be exercised contrary to the purposes and principles of the United Nations.

Article 30
Nothing in this Declaration may be interpreted as implying for any State, group or person any right to engage in any activity or to perform any act aimed at the destruction of any of the rights and freedoms set forth herein.

Adopted and proclaimed by General Assembly Resolution 217A (III) of 10 December 1948.

Document 5: China's Gulag

In an interview with Freedom Review, *Harry Wu describes his life in a labor camp in Communist China and why he believes the United States overlooks human rights violations because of its need for Chinese goods.*

Since 1989 the world has gotten many surprises from the Chinese government: China supports North Korea. It sells missiles to Pakistan. It arrests me, a citizen of the U.S. It launches missiles close to Taiwan. . . .

It's time to ask: What is the China policy of the United States? The Pentagon has forces in the Middle East, in South America. But if something were to happen with China, there is no plan.

Harry Wu, "Out of the Chinese Gulag," by Al Santoli, *Freedom Review*, November/December 1995, p. 46.

Document 6: Supporting South African Democracy

An excerpt from Nelson Mandela's speech to a joint session of the U.S. Congress describes the wretched lives South Africans face under apartheid. Mandela pleads for American support to help South Africa build a democratic society.

To deny any person their human rights is to challenge their very humanity. To impose on them a wretched life of hunger and deprivation is to dehumanize them. But such has been the terrible fate of all black persons in our country under the system of apartheid.

The extent of the deprivation of millions of people has to be seen to be believed. The injury is made more intolerable by the opulence of our white compatriots and the deliberate distortion of the economy to feed that opulence.

The process of the reconstruction of South African society must and will also entail the transformation of its economy. We need a strong and growing economy. We require an economy that is able to address the needs of all the people of our country; that can provide food, houses, education, health services, social security, and everything that makes human life human, that makes life joyful and not a protracted encounter with hopelessness and despair.

We believe that the fact of the apartheid structure of the South African economy and the enormous and pressing needs of the people make it inevitable that the democratic government will intervene in this economy, acting through the elected parliament. We have put the matter to the business community of our country that the need for a public sector is one of the elements in a many-sided strategy of economic development and restructuring that has to be considered by us all, including the private sector. . . .

We shall need your support to achieve the postapartheid economic objectives which are an intrinsic part of the process of the restoration of the human rights of the people of South Africa. We would like to approach the issue of our economic cooperation not as a relationship between donor and recipient, between a dependent and a benefactor. . . .

To destroy racism in the world, we together must expunge apartheid racism in South Africa. Justice and liberty must be our tool, prosperity and happiness our weapon.

Address to the Joint Session of the Houses of Congress of the USA, Washington, DC, June 26, 1990.

Document 7: The Tibetan Struggle

In a speech delivered on the fortieth anniversary of the Tibetan National Uprising, Tenzin Gyatso, the fourteenth Dalai Lama, discusses the racial and cultural discrimination that causes suffering for the people of Tibet.

Although some development and economic progress has been made in Tibet [since China took control], our country continues to face many fundamental problems. In terms of history, culture, language, religion, way of life and geographical conditions, there are stark differences between Tibet and China. These differences result in grave clashes of values, dissent and distrust. At the sight of the slightest dissent the Chinese authorities react with force and repression resulting in widespread and serious violations of human rights in Tibet. These abuses of rights have a distinct character, and are aimed at preventing Tibetans as a people from asserting their own identity and culture, and their wish to preserve them. Thus, human rights violations in Tibet are often the result of policies of racial and cultural discrimination and are only the symptoms and consequences of a deeper problem. The Chinese authorities identify the distinct culture and religion of Tibet as the root cause of Tibetan resentment and dissent. Hence their policies are aimed at decimating this integral core of the Tibetan civilization and identity. . . .

The plight of the Tibetan people and our non-violent freedom struggle has touched the hearts and conscience of all people who cherish truth and justice. The international awareness of the issue of Tibet has reached an unprecedented height since [1998]. Concerns and active support for Tibet are not confined to human rights organizations, governments and parliaments. Universities, schools, religious and social groups, artistic and business communities as well as people from many other walks of life have also come to understand the problem of Tibet and are now expressing their solidarity with our cause. Reflecting this rising popular sentiment, many governments and parliaments have made the problem of Tibet an important issue on the agenda of their relations with the government of China. . . .

With my homage to the brave men and women of Tibet, who have died for the cause of our freedom, I pray for an early end to the suffering of our people.

Tenzin Gyatso, "China and Human Rights." Speech delivered to the 39th Anniversary of the Tibetan National Uprising, Dharamsala, India, March 10, 1998.

Document 8: On Gandhi's Death

Jawaharlal Nehru, prime minister of India, spoke the following words expressing his grief over the assassination of Mohandas Gandhi. He encouraged Indians to carry on the ideals that Gandhi represented.

Friends and comrades, the light has gone out of our lives and there is darkness everywhere. I do not know what to tell you and how to say it. Our beloved leader, Bapu as we called him, the father of the nation, is no more. Perhaps I am wrong to say that. Nevertheless, we will not see him again as we have seen him for these many years. We will not run to him for advice and seek solace from him, and that is a terrible blow, not to me only, but to millions and millions in this country, and it is a little difficult to soften the blow by any other advice that I or anyone else can give you.

The light has gone out, I said, and yet I was wrong. For the light that shone in this country was no ordinary light.

The light that has illumined this country for these many years will illumine this country for many more years, and a thousand years later that light will still be seen in this country and the world will see it and it will give solace to innumerable hearts. For that light represented the living truth . . . the eternal truths, reminding us of the right path, drawing us from error, taking this ancient country to freedom.

All this has happened when there was so much more for him to do. We could never think that he was unnecessary or that he had done his task. But now, particularly, when we are faced with so many difficulties, his not being with us is a blow most terrible to bear.

A madman has put an end to his life, for I can only call him mad who did it, and yet there has been enough of poison spread in this country during the past years and months, and this poison has had effect on people's minds. We must face this poison, we must root out this poison, and we must face all the perils that encompass us and face them not madly or badly but rather in the way that our beloved teacher taught us to face them. The first thing to remember now is that no one of us dare misbehave because we are angry. We have to behave like strong and determined people, determined to face all the perils that surround us, determined to carry out the mandate that our great teacher and our great leader has given us, remembering always that if, as I believe, his spirit looks upon us and sees us, nothing would displease his soul so much as to see that we have indulged in any small behaviour or any violence.

Jawaharlal Nehru, "The Light Has Gone Out of Our Lives." Speech given in Delhi, India, January 30, 1948.

Document 9: The Result of Our Work

In the following letter to President Harry S. Truman dated June 21, 1949, Eleanor Roosevelt highlights the results of her work as chairwoman of the UN Commission on Human Rights.

Dear Mr. President:

I want first to thank you for the opportunities you have

given me to work on the Human Rights Commission. The session closed last night.

Realizing that you probably do not want to be bothered by a personal report at the present time, I am writing this, though, of course, if you want me to come to Washington I shall do so.

The result of our work is only the first draft of the Covenant. We discussed only political and civil rights. The document which will go to the governments, however, will be accompanied by different plans for ways of enforcing the rights that are to be accepted in the final Covenant.

Our only plan is a joint plan with the United Kingdom and it will go forward with the others. This is the only thing on which we were able to agree with the United Kingdom. I have never known them to be so uncooperative as they were in this session. . . . It was unfortunate especially because in previous sessions we have been able to get together with the United Kingdom on many situations.

Needless to say we practically never agreed with the USSR, and they felt that the document was a very poor one because the economic and social rights were not really discussed and are going to governments simply as additional articles for comment by governments.

One of the things we shall have to decide before the next meeting is whether in this Covenant we shall include any of these rights. Many of our people in this country lean toward the belief that civil and political rights without some measure of economic and social rights, have comparatively little value but these are new rights to many governments and must be approached gradually. Whether we wish to deal with economic and social rights in a second Covenant to follow the first one, or whether we wish to include them in separate protocols which nations can ratify one by one as they find the atmosphere of their countries favorable, are the questions before us. These must be decided as far as our attitude is concerned before the next meeting.

Steve Neal, *Eleanor and Harry: The Correspondence of Eleanor Roosevelt and Harry S. Truman.* New York: Scribner, 2002, pp. 162–63.

Document 10: A Lifelong Commitment

Blanche Wiesen Cook outlines Eleanor Roosevelt's dedication and lifelong commitment to making life better for others.

Fifty years after ER [Eleanor Roosevelt] worked to place human rights on the international agenda, the Universal Declaration of Human Rights, adopted by the United Nations on 10 December 1948, [which states that] every individual, citizen, committee, and nation is responsible and accountable [and] encouraged to protest human rights abuses, empowered to prevent ethnic cleansing, torture, lynchings, hate crimes, and genocide. . . .

To contemplate ER's life of example and responsibility is to forestall gloom. She understood, above all, that politics is not an isolated individualist adventure. She sought alliances, created community, worked with movements for justice and peace. Against great odds, and under terrific pressure, she refused to withdraw from controversy. She brought her network of agitators and activists into the White House, and never considered a political setback a permanent defeat. She enjoyed the game, and weathered the abuse. Energized by her friends and allies, she devoted some part of every day to the business of making life better for most people. To contemplate her life of action and determination is to reconsider the role of popular movements everywhere growing, reorganizing, still and again dedicated to a politics of care, love, and justice.

Blanche Wiesen Cook, *Eleanor Roosevelt*, vol. 2. New York: Viking, 1999, pp. 6–8.

Document 11: Roosevelt's Influence

In a letter to the sultan of Morocco, Muhammad V, dated July 31, 1956, Eleanor Roosevelt pleads for more than ten thousand Jews to be released from refugee camps in Morocco and other Arab states and allowed to immigrate to Israel.

Your Majesty:

I wish to acknowledge your kind message transmitted to me through your representative. It is very gratifying to know that you remember my husband's visit to you. He often told me of that visit and of his hopes that some day you would bring back much of your desert into fertile land through the use of underground water which might be found, and he recalled his advice to you never to give away all of your oil rights since you would need a substantial amount of those rights to bring this water to the surface. To have you remember this and his interest in the welfare of these areas was very gratifying to me.

As you know, my husband had a great interest in bringing to people in general throughout the world better conditions for living. We tried to do this for the people of the United States, but he was also anxious to see it come about in the world as a whole.

I have had an appeal to bring to your attention the fact that there is a group of very poor Jewish people now in camps in Morocco who were to have been allowed to leave for Israel. They are of no value to the future development of Morocco as they have not succeeded in building for themselves a suitable economy. However, Israel can perhaps help them to develop skills and to improve their lot. Your government has given assurances that they would be allowed to leave but when it has come to a point in the last few months the actual necessary deeds to accomplish their departure have not been forthcoming.

I am sure that it is Your Majesty's desire, as it was my husband's, not only to see better conditions for your own people but to see people throughout the world improve their condition. I hope Morocco will show the world that she is committed, as I believe she is, to the freedom of people who are living there which must include the freedom of people to emigrate. The Jews who had no country now have Israel where they can take their less fortunate brethren and help them to a better way of life. It seems to me that the Arab states would be forwarding their own interests if they were to make this transfer possible. It would relieve the Arab states of indigent people and would show the world that they did have an interest in helping unfortunate people to improve themselves. I, therefore, bring this situation to your attention in this note which primarily expresses my gratitude for your memory of my husband, since I believe that you would not have remembered my husband if you did not have somewhat similar aims.

Very sincerely yours,
Eleanor Roosevelt

Joseph P. Lash, *Eleanor: The Years Alone.* New York: W.W. Norton, 1972, p. 339.

Document 12: A Parody

Frederick Douglass penned the following parody of religion in the South, where he saw piety and hypocrisy abound, particularly among the slaveholders.

Come, saints and sinners, hear me tell
How pious priests whip Jack and Nell,
And women buy and children sell,
And preach all sinners down to hell,
And sing of heavenly union.

They'll bleat and baa, dona like goats,
Gorge down black sheep, and strain at motes,
Array their backs in fine black coats,
Then seize their negroes by their throats,
And choke, for heavenly union.

They'll church you if you sip a dram,
And damn you if you steal a lamb;
Yet rob old Tony, Doll, and Sam,
Of human rights, and bread and ham;
Kidnapper's heavenly union.

They'll loudly talk of Christ's reward,
And bind his image with a cord,
And scold, and swing the lash abhorred,
And sell their brother in the Lord
To handcuffed heavenly union.

They'll read and sing a sacred song,

And make a prayer both loud and long,
And teach the right and do the wrong,
Hailing the brother, sister throng,
With words of heavenly union.

We wonder how such saints can sing,
Or praise the Lord upon the wing,
Who roar, and scold, and whip, and sting,
And to their slaves and mammon cling,
In guilty conscience union.

They'll raise tobacco, corn, and rye,
And drive, and thieve, and cheat, and lie,
And lay up treasures in the sky,
By making switch and cowskin fly,
In hope of heavenly union.

They'll crack old Tony on the skull,
And preach and roar like Bashan bull,
Or braying ass, of mischief full,
Then seize old Jacob by the wool,
And pull for heavenly union.

A roaring, ranting, sleek man-thief,
Who lived on mutton, veal, and beef,
Yet never would afford relief
To needy, sable sons of grief,
Was big with heavenly union.

"Love not the world," the preacher said,
And winked his eye, and shook his head;
He seized on Tom, and Dick, and Ned,
Cut short their meat, and clothes, and bread,
Yet still loved heavenly union.

Another preacher whining spoke
Of One whose heart for sinners broke:
He tied old Nanny to an oak,
And drew the blood at every stroke,

And prayed for heavenly union.
Two others oped their iron jaws,
And waved their children-stealing paws;
There sat their children in gewgaws;
By stinting negroes' backs and maws,
They kept up heavenly union.

All good from Jack another takes,
And entertains their flirts and rakes,
Who dress as sleek as glossy snakes,
And cram their mouths with sweetened cakes;
And this goes down for union.

Frederick Douglass, *Narrative of the Life of Frederick Douglass, an American Slave, Written by Himself*. Boston: Anti-Slavery Office, 1845.

For Further Research

Books on Human Rights

Maurice W. Cranston, *What Are Human Rights?* New York: BasicBooks, 1962.

Kerry Kennedy Cuomo, *Speak Truth to Power: Human Rights Defenders Who Are Changing Our World.* New York: Crown, 2000.

Robert F. Drinan, *Cry of the Oppressed: The History and Hope of the Human Rights Revolution.* San Francisco: Harper & Row, 1987.

Eileen Lucas, *Contemporary Human Rights Activists.* New York: Facts On File, 1997.

David Selby, *Human Rights.* Cambridge, UK: Cambridge University Press, 1987.

Books with Biographical Information

Jimmy Carter

Jimmy Carter, *Keeping Faith: Memoirs of a President.* New York: Bantam Books, 1982.

——, *Living Faith.* New York: Times Books, 1996.

——, *Talking Peace: A Vision for the Next Generation.* New York: Dutton Children's Books, 1993.

Joshua Muravchik, *The Uncertain Crusade: Jimmy Carter and the Dilemmas of Human Rights Policy.* Lanham, MD: Hamilton, 1986.

Frederick Douglass

John W. Blassingame, ed., *The Frederick Douglass Papers.* New Haven, CT: Yale University Press, 1979.

Arna Bontemps, *Free at Last: The Life of Frederick Douglass.* New York: Dodd, Mead, 1971.

Frederick Douglass, *Frederick Douglass: Selected Speeches and Writings.* Chicago: Lawrence Hill Books, 1999.

Mohandas Gandhi

Mohandas Gandhi, *All Men Are Brothers.* New York: Columbia University Press, 1958.

——, *An Autobiography: The Story of My Experiments with Truth.* Boston: Beacon, 1957.

——, *The Essential Gandhi: An Anthology.* Ed. by Louis Fischer. New York: Random House, 1962.

——, *Non-Violent Resistance.* New York: Schocken Books, 1951.

Gerald Gold, *Gandhi: A Pictorial Biography.* New York: NewMarket, 1983.

Robert Payne, *The Life and Death of Mahatma Gandhi.* New York: Dutton, 1969.

Catherine Owens Peare, *Gandhi: Father of Non-Violence.* San Francisco: Hawthorne, 1969.

Stanley A. Wolpert, *Gandhi's Passion: The Life and Legacy of Mahatma Gandhi.* New York: Oxford University Press, 2001.

Tenzin Gyatso

Tenzin Gyatso, *Essential Teachings: His Holiness the Dalai Lama.* Ed. by Marianne Dresser. Berkeley, CA: North Atlantic Books, 1995.

——, *Freedom in Exile: The Autobiography of the Dalai Lama.* New York: HarperCollins, 1990.

Natasa Kandic

Kerry Kennedy Cuomo, *Speak Truth to Power: Human Rights Defenders Who Are Changing Our World*. New York: Crown, 2000.

Martin Luther King Jr.

Martin Luther King Jr., *The Autobiography of Martin Luther King Jr.* Ed. by Clayborne Carson. New York: Warner Books, 1998.

———, *A Call to Conscience: The Landmark Speeches of Martin Luther King Jr.* Ed. by Clayborne Carson and Kris Shepard. New York: Warner Books, 2001.

———, *I have a Dream.* San Francisco: HarperSanFrancisco, 1993.

Nelson Mandela

Nelson Mandela, *Long Walk to Freedom.* Boston: Little, Brown, 1994.

———, *Nelson Mandela Speaks: Forging a Democratic, Non-Racial South Africa.* Ed. by Steve Clark. New York: Pathfinder, 1993.

Martin Meredith, *Nelson Mandela: A Biography.* New York: St. Martin's, 1998.

Eva Perón

Tomás Eloy Martínez, *Santa Evita.* New York: Knopf, 1996.

Eleanor Roosevelt

Blanche Wiesen Cook, *Eleanor Roosevelt: The Defining Years, vol. 2, 1933–1938.* New York: Viking, 1999.

Joseph P. Lash, *Eleanor: The Years Alone.* New York: W.W. Norton, 1972.

Eleanor Roosevelt, *Empty Without You: The Intimate Letters of*

Eleanor Roosevelt and Lorena Hickok. New York: Free Press, 1998.

Ann Weil, *Eleanor Roosevelt: Fighter for Social Justice.* New York: Aladdin Books, 1989.

Harry Wu

Hongda Harry Wu, *Laogai: The Chinese Gulag.* New York: Westview, 1992.

Hongda Harry Wu and Carolyn Wakeman, *Bitter Winds: A Memoir of My Years in China's Gulag.* New York: Wiley, 1995.

Hongda Harry Wu and George Vecsey, *Troublemaker: One Man's Crusade Against China's Cruelty.* New York: Times Books, 1996.

Books on Human Rights Organizations

Amnesty International

Ann Marie Clark, *Diplomacy of Conscience: Amnesty International and Changing Human Rights Norms.* Princeton, NJ: Princeton University Press, 2001.

Robert F. Drinan, *The Mobilization of Shame: A World View of Human Rights.* New Haven, CT: Yale University Press, 2001.

Egon Larsen, *A Flame in Barbed Wire: The Story of Amnesty International.* New York: Norton, 1979.

Jonathan Power, *Amnesty International: The Human Rights Story.* New York: McGraw-Hill, 1981.

Marie Staunton and Sally Fenn, *The Amnesty International Handbook.* Claremont, CA: Hunter House, 1991.

The United Nations

Clark M. Eichelberger, *UN: The First Twenty Years.* New York: Harper & Row, 1965.

Periodicals

Jimmy Carter

Millard Grimes, "The 39th President," *Georgia Trend*, January 2000.

Faith McLellan, "Jimmy Carter and Life After the US Presidency," *Lancet*, March 29, 2003.

Kenneth T. Walsh, "Peace Laureate," *U.S. News & World Report*, October 21, 2002.

Mohandas Gandhi

Judith Brown, "Gandhi and Nehru: Frustrated Visionaries?" *History Today*, September 1, 1997.

James Douglass, "Jesus, Gandhi, King Point the Way," *National Catholic Reporter*, September 28, 2001.

Nelson Mandela, "The Sacred Warrior," *Time*, December 31, 1999.

Tenzin Gyatso: Dalai Lama

Dorothy Rompalske, "The Power of One," *Biography*, January 1999.

Kenneth Woodward, "A Lama to the Globe," *Newsweek*, August 16, 1999.

Natasa Kandic

Dejan Anastasijevic, "At War Against War Crimes," *Time International*, April 28, 2003.

Nelson Mandela

John Battersby, "Mandela," *Christian Science Monitor*, February 10, 2000.

C. Stone Brown, "The Life and Times of Nelson Mandela," *Crisis*, January/February 2000.

Petter Hain, "I Feel Only Stillness," *New Statesman*, November 1, 1996.

Iqbal Masih

Pharis J. Harvey, "Iqbal's Death," *Christian Century*, May 24, 1995.

Timothy Ryan, "Iqbal Masih's Life—a Call to Human Rights Vigilance," *Christian Science Monitor*, May 3, 1995.

Eva Perón

Amber Becker, "Argentina Diva," *New Moon*, July/August 2002.

Michael Neill and Laura Sanderson Healy, "Evita," *People*, December 12, 1996.

Mary Robinson

Sally Alderson, "Taking Hold Boldly," *Swiss World*, April/May 1999.

Aisha Labi, "Mary Robinson: Humanitarian, 55," *Time International*, September 13, 1999.

Eleanor Roosevelt

Adam Fifield, "Women Reformers," *New York Times*, June 3, 2001.

Mary Glendon, "A World Made New: Eleanor Roosevelt and the Universal Declaration of Human Rights," *Human Rights Quarterly*, February 2002.

Doris Kearns Goodwin, "Eleanor Roosevelt," *Time*, April 13, 1998.

Mark Mazower, "Eleanor Roosevelt," *New Statesman*, February 2002.

Harry Wu

Stephen Goode, "Wu Decries U.S. Denial of Chinese Crackdown," *Insight on the News*, January 24, 2000.

Anthony C. LoBaido, "Harry Wu on the Real China," *WorldNetDaily*, April 5, 2001. www.worldnetdaily.com.

Cynthia Sanz, "Rebel with a Cause: Human Rights Gadfly," *People Weekly*, September 11, 1995.

Web Sites

Amnesty International, www.amnesty.org. This site provides information on human rights activists, work, and needs around the world and offers links to other sites.

Human Rights Organizations & Resources, www.hrweb. org/resource.html. This Web site lists human rights organizations, activists, and research organizations.

Human Rights Watch, www.hrw.org. Current events, campaigns, commentaries, crises, and worldwide activities are detailed on this Web site.

Reebok Human Rights Foundation, www.reebok.com. This site provides information on human rights activists and their work around the world as well as annual human rights award winners.

Speak Truth to Power, www.speaktruth.org. This site offers information on human rights activists and their international work.

United Nations, www.un.org/rights. This site provides detailed treaties, current human rights news, incidents, proceedings, and the Universal Declaration of Human Rights.

Index

abolitionists. *See* antislavery movement
activists, 11–13
  activities of, 13–15
  contributions of, 18–19
  motivations of, 16–18
  suppression of, 16
  see also specific activists
African Americans, 54
African National Congress (ANC), 55–56
  Mandela and, 63–64
  moral high ground of, 66
  pacifist philosophy of, 56
  success of, 63
  work of, to end apartheid, 73–77
  see also MK Policy
African National Congress Youth League (ANCYL), 56–57, 58, 73
African Union, 131–32
Amnesty International (AI)
  financing of, 189–90
  founding of, 186, 188–89
  mission of, 186, 187
  work of, 12–13
Anastasijevic, Dejan, 172
Anderson, Marian, 120
Annan, Kofi, 128
Anthony, Aaron, 88
Anthony, Susan B.

early life of, 98–99
later years of, 102
temperance movement and, 99–100
women's movement and, 100–102
anti-Semitism, 138
antislavery convention, 184
antislavery movement
  Frederick Douglass's work in, 86–87, 90–94
  Susan B. Anthony's work in, 100
Anti-Slavery Society, 100
apartheid
  beginnings of, 56
  defeat of, Nelson Mandela and, 54, 61
  international efforts to end, 77
  work of ANC to end, 73–77
Argentina, 121–26
Atlanta Project, 298
Auld, Sophia, 89
Auld, Thomas, 95

Bailey, Frederick. *See* Douglass, Frederick
Baker, Eric, 188
Bambata Rebellion, 33
Bantustan policy, 57–58

Battersby, John, 62
Becker, Amber, 124
Begin, Menachem, 196
Benenson, Peter, 186, 188
Blom-Cooper, Louis, 188
Boers, 24
bonded labor, 109–14, 184
Bonded Labor Liberation
  Foundation (BLLF), 109,
  110–13
Bornemann, Thomas, 204
Bosnia, 170–76
Brazil, 131
Brinkley, Douglas, 200
Britain, Indian
  independence movement
  and, 25–30
Brown, C. Stone, 53
Brown, John, 92
Buddha, 43, 48
Burma (Myanmar), 193

Cambodia, 130
Camp David Peace Accords,
  196
Carter, Jimmy
  as governor, 194–95
  postpresidential career of,
  198–99
  presidency of, 196–98
Carter, Rosalynn, 204
Carter Center and Library,
  195, 200–205
Catholic Justice and Peace
  Commission, 11–12
child labor, 109–14
Chile, 192
China
  Communist takeover of,
  154–57
  crackdown in, 193

after death of Mao, 160–61
Laogai prison system in,
  157–60, 165–68
takeover of Tibet by, 10,
  146
Tiananmen Square
  massacre in, 13–14
Universal Declaration of
  Human Rights and, 130
Citizens Commission on
  Human Rights, 12–13
civil rights movement
  Eleanor Roosevelt and,
  120
  King and, 104–108
Civil War, 92–93
college courses, 15
Communist Party, 154–57,
  160–61
Conniff, Richard, 84
convention, on the rights of
  the child, 130–31
Convention on the Political
  Rights of Women, 183–84
Cook, Blanche Wiesen, 118
Croatia, 170–71
Cuomo, Kerry Kennedy,
  169

Dalai Lama. See Gyatso,
  Tenzin
Daniels, Eddie, 66
Daughters of Temperance,
  99
Daughters of the American
  Revolution (DAR), 120
Defiance Campaign, 73
de Klerk, F.W., 77
Douglass, Anna, 90, 91–92,
  95
Douglass, Frederick

during Civil War, 92–93
early life of, 85, 88–90
in Europe, 91
"Lessons of the Hour"
  speech by, 96–97
life of, as slave, 85–86
self-education of, 89
work of, in antislavery
  movement, 86–87, 90–94
Dred Scott decision, 60

East Timor, 14–15, 64,
  130–31
Eichelberger, Clark M., 178
Einstein, Albert, 22
El Salvador, 193
Emancipation
  Proclamation, 93
Ethical Globalization
  Initiative, 131
European Convention for
  the Protection of Human
  Rights, 181
Eva Perón Foundation,
  124–25

Federal Bureau of
  Investigation (FBI), 107
feminist movement. *See*
  women's movement
Fenn, Sally, 186
Fifteenth Amendment,
  93–94
Foege, William, 205
forced labor. *See* bonded
  labor
Freedman's Bank, 94
freedom, 16
Frick, Kevin, 204

Gandhi, Kasturbi, 23, 29

Gandhi, Mohandas, 38
assassination of, 22, 30
contributions of, 18, 44–45
economic principles of, 33,
  36–37, 49–50
Indian independence
  movement and, 25–30, 35
King's admiration for, 105
noncooperation strategy
  of, 31–32
nonviolence principles of,
  26–27, 32–35
passive resistance strategy
  of, 23–24
politics of, 49–51
on religion, 40–41, 43
self-sufficiency principle
  of, 34
in South Africa, 23–25,
  41–42
truths taught by, 45–48
Garrison, William Lloyd,
  90
Garvey, Marcus, 56
Genocide Convention, 183
Global Fund for Women,
  132
globalization, 136
Godse, Nathuram, 22
governmental abuses, 15–16
Government of India Act, 28
governments
  accountability of, 129
  scores of, 184–85
grassroots campaigns,
  130–31
Green, Shields, 92
Griffiths, Julia, 91
Grimes, Millard, 194
guinea worm programme,
  202–203

Gumede, Josiah, 56
Gyatso, Tenzin (Dalai Lama)
  Chinese position of, 150, 155
  early life of, 144–46
  exile of, 141–43, 146–48
  finding of new Dalai Lama and, 149–50
  qualities of, 151
  Tibetan Buddhism and, 148–49

Harpers Ferry, West Virginia, 92
hartal, 41
Harvey, Pharis J., 112
Havel, Vaclav, 192
Healy, Laura Sanderson, 121
Hertzog, J.B., 56
honor killings, 12
Hoover, J. Edgar, 107
Hopkins, Donald, 202
Humanitarian Law Center, 169
Humanitarian Legal Center, 12
Human Rights Watch, 13
Humphreys, Christmas, 148
Husseini, Rana, 12

India
  democracy in, 22
  partition of, 30, 35
  see also Gandhi, Mohandas
Indian National Congress, 26, 27
International Criminal Court, 137–38
Iraq, 193

issues
  exposure of, 13–15
  government obstacles to, 15–16
  increasing visibility of, 134–35
  most significant, 129
  state of, 192–93
Iyer, Pico, 141

Jalianwala Bagh, 42–43
Jesus Christ, 43, 105
Jinnah, Mohammed Ali, 27, 29
John XXIII (pope), 180
Jordan, honor killings in, 12
journalists, 12
Jung, Carolyn, 158

Kandic, Natasa, 12, 169–76
King, Martin Luther, Jr.
  assassination of, 108
  civil rights movement and, 104–108
  early life of, 104–105
  "I have a dream" speech of, 107–108
  on religion, 105–106
  on Vietnam War, 108
Kosovo, 170–76
Kuwait, 193

Labi, Aisha, 134
Labor Today (journal), 116
Laogai prison system, 157–61, 165–68
lawyers, 11–12
Leathem, Rebecca, 21
"Lessons of the Hour, The" (Frederick Douglass), 96–97

letter-writing campaigns,
13, 187–91
Liberia, 11–12
*Life and Death of Mahatma
Gandhi* (Payne), 35
Lincoln, Abraham, 92–93
LoBaido, Anthony C., 153
Lockerbie (Scotland), 64–65
Long Walk to Freedom
(Nelson Mandela), 60, 69,
75–76
Lucas, Nance, 127

Machel, Graca, 78
Madikizela, Winnie
Nomzamo. *See* Mandela,
Winnie
Malan, Daniel, 73
Mandela, Nelson, 31, 79
ANC and, 63–64
ANCYL and, 57, 73
arrest of, 59–60
biographical information,
54–55, 72–73
contributions of, 18
criticism of, 66
early political activism of,
55–59, 73–74
elected president of South
Africa, 77–78
end of apartheid and, 54,
61, 73–77
on Gandhi, 31–37
on human rights progress,
79–82
international support of,
77
Middle East peace talks by,
64
MK Policy and, 58–59,
74–75

prison and
influence of, 62–70
release from, 192
sentenced to, 60–61, 75
on reconciliation and
forgiveness, 65–68
on religion, 70–71
on South Africa, before
colonization, 53–54
Mandela (Sampson), 67
Mandela, Winnie, 58, 74,
76, 78
Mandela Children's Fund,
65
Mandela Plan, 57
Martínez, Tomás Eloy, 124
Marx, Karl, 49
Marxism, 155
Masih, Iqbal, 18, 109–14
Mbeki, Thabo, 78
McGill, Sara Ann, 98
McLellan, Faith, 200
Méndez, Juan, 15
Middle East peace talks, 64,
196
Milosevic, Slobodan,
169–70
MK Policy, 58–59, 74–75
Moldovan, Russel, 103
Montgomery Improvement
Association, 105–106
Mountbatten, Louis, 22,
29–30
Mueller, Bobby, 18
Murray, Anna. *See*
Douglass, Anna
Muslim League, 27, 29
Myanmar (Burma), 193

Narain, Jai Prakash, 49
Narrative of the Life of

Frederick Douglass
(Frederick Douglass), 88
National American
  Women's Suffrage
  Association (NAWSA),
  101, 102
National Consumer's
  League, 117
National Volunteer Corps,
  26
Nehru, Jawaharlal, 26–29,
  45, 51
Neill, Michael, 121
Nineteenth Amendment, 102
Noll, Mark, 104
nonviolent civil
  disobedience
  of Gandhi, 26–27, 32–35
  of King, 105
North Star (newspaper), 91

100 Flowers Movement,
  155–56
Ortiz, Alicia Dujovne, 123
Ortizan, Dianna, 17–18

Pakistan
  bonded child labor in,
    109–14
  creation of, 30
Panchen Lama, 149
Parks, Rosa, 105
passive resistance, 23–24,
  26–27, 32–35
Payne, Robert, 35
Perkins, Frances, 119
Perón, Eva
  early life of, 122–23
  wealth acquired by, 126
  work of, on behalf of poor,
    123–26

Perón, Juan, 121–26
Pitts, Helen, 95
police abuses, 134–36
poverty
  as biggest threat to society,
    70, 80–82
  Eva Perón's work to
    reduce, 123–26
Program of Action, 56–57,
  73
public demonstrations,
  13–14
public education, 14

Ramos-Horta, José, 14–15
Rauschenbusch, Walter, 105
Ray, James Earl, 108
Reconstruction, 101
river blindness, 203
Rivonia Trial, 75, 77
Robinson, Mary
  on major issues, 129–30
  political achievements of,
    127–28
  as role model for women,
    131–32
  as UN High
    Commissioner for
    Human Rights, 127–28,
    133–35
Roosevelt, Eleanor, 116–20,
  132–33
Roosevelt, Franklin, 117, 119
Ryan, James, 72
Ryan, Timothy, 109

Sadat, Anwar, 196
Sakharov, Andrey, 18
Sampson, Anthony, 67
satyagraha. *See* passive
  resistance

self-sufficiency, 34
September 11, 2001, 136, 138–39
Sharpeville Massacre, 75
Sisulu, Walter, 55, 66–67
slavery
  in Middle East, 185
  realities of, 85–86, 88
Smith, Adam, 34
Smuts, Jan, 25, 41
Snow, Edgar, 44
Social Aid Foundation, 125
socialism, 49–50
South Africa
  apartheid policy in, 54, 56, 61, 73–77
  Gandhi's influence on, 32
  Gandhi's work in, 23–25, 41–42
  map of, 57
  oppression of blacks in, 57–58
  see also Mandela, Nelson
Southern Christian Leadership Conference (SCLC), 106
Soviet Union, 192
spinning wheel, 26–27
Stanton, Elizabeth Cady, 86, 100–102
Staunton, Marie, 186
Steyn, Douw, 69
Sudan, 15
suffrage movement, 100–102
swadeshi, 34

temperance movement, 99–100
terrorism, 129, 136–38
Tiananmen Square

massacre, 13–14
Tibet
  Chinese aggression against, 146, 150
  Dalai Lama's efforts to save, 141–52
Tibetan Buddhism, 148–49
trade sanctions, 13
Transvaal Indians, 24
Truth and Reconciliation Commission, 77–78
Tworkov, Helen, 144

UN Commission on Human Rights, 178–85
  see also Universal Declaration of Human Rights
Universal Declaration of Human Rights
  adoption of, 179–82
  Amnesty International and, 191–92
  Eleanor Roosevelt and, 116, 132–33
  implementation of, 182–83
  nations' observance of, 184–85
university courses, 15
untouchables, 26
Ustinov, Peter, 68

Vietnam War, 108
Voice of the Martyrs, 13
Volcker, Paul, 197

Walsh, Kenneth T., 197
war on terrorism, 129, 136–38
Washington, D.C., civil rights march on, 107–108

Wells, Ida B., 95–96
women, role models for,
  131–33
women's movement
  Frederick Douglass and, 87
  Susan B. Anthony and,
    100–102
Women's Trade Union
  League, 117
Woodhull, Victoria,
  101–102
Woods, Samuel Kofi, 11–12,
  16
working conditions,
  inhumane, 109–14
Works Progress
  Administration (WPA),

120
World Organization Against
  Torture, 13
World War II, 29, 120
Wu, Ching-Lee, 165
Wu, Harry
  in Communist China,
    154–57
  motivation of, 158
  release of, from prison,
    160–63
  in U.S., 162–64
  see also Laogai prison
    system

Yugoslavia, 12, 134–35,
  169–76, 192